DO NOT REMOVE
CARDS FROM POCKET

Pinstripe Pandemonium

Pinstripe Pandemonium

A SEASON WITH THE NEW YORK YANKEES

GEOFFREY STOKES

1817

HARPER & ROW, PUBLISHERS, New York

CAMBRIDGE, PHILADELPHIA, SAN FRANCISCO, LONDON
MEXICO CITY, SÃO PAULO, SYDNEY

Portions of this work originally appeared in *The Village Voice*. PINSTRIPE PAN-
DEMONIUM. Copyright © 1984 by Geoffrey Stokes. All rights reserved. Printed in the
United States of America. No part of this book may be used or reproduced in any
manner whatsoever without written permission except in the case of brief quotations
embodied in critical articles and reviews. For information address Harper & Row,
Publishers, Inc., 10 East 53rd Street, New York, N.Y. 10022. Published simultaneously
in Canada by Fitzhenry & Whiteside Limited, Toronto.

FIRST EDITION

Designer: Helene Berinsky

Library of Congress Cataloging in Publication Data

Stokes, Geoffrey.
    Pinstripe pandemonium.

    1. New York Yankees (Baseball team) I. Title.
GV875.N4S76   1984   796.357'64'097471   83–48806
ISBN 0–06–015311–3

84 85 86 87 88 10 9 8 7 6 5 4 3 2 1

5000001

For, in order of appearance, the Yankee fan, the Red Sox rooter, and the little girl who rose as the horses barreled into the stretch at Belmont and shouted— apparently in the belief that this was what one *did* at sporting events—"Let's go, Mets!"

Contents

< vii >

Foreword

The baseball diamond isn't quite forever, but it is close enough. By the time Chicago won the first National League pennant, in 1876, the game had been around for a generation; the time when baseball didn't exist now lies beyond the reach of the American memory. Though there are differences, still, among the parks—Fenway with so many crags and juts the Brooklyn Democratic organization might have designed it, the indoor Kingdome with its short, high fences and eerie sound effects—the diamond itself is a reassuring constant. Willie Randolph runs to first in Babe Ruth's footsteps, Ruth ran in Willie Keeler's.

The diamond is public space, available for the price of a ticket. By contrast, the clubhouse is a mystery. Private, even secret, the Yankee clubhouse is at the head of a ramp fifty feet and an entire world away from the playing field.

There is a carpet on its floor, but as a hangout for young millionaires the Yankee clubhouse is on the Spartan side. Located in the cellar beneath the Stadium's first-base box seats, the clubhouse has, in addition to the locker room, a players' lounge, a trainer's room, showers and lavatories, the manager's office, and a supply and laundry room. The largest of these—and the room one enters from the

< ix >

main door—is the locker room. A rectangle roughly forty feet by a hundred, its available wall space is taken up by doorless cubicles that the players and coaches call home for about six months a year.

Each is about three feet wide and contains, against the back wall, a lockable storage box whose padded top makes it imaginably usable as a bench, a rod and some hooks for hanging clothes, and a couple of shelves. Since the clothing rods are located directly over the storage boxes, these are almost never used as benches, and the players sit instead on mass-produced steel and plastic chairs in front of their lockers.

In addition to these chairs, the room is furnished with two battered tables flanked by picnic benches. The first of these, located in about the middle of the room, is usually occupied by Pete Sheehey, who has worked in the Yankee clubhouse since the days of Babe Ruth. The second, toward the rear, is used for the pregame distribution of tickets and the postgame distribution of food. Until the batboys take them out for batting practice, a couple of supermarket shopping carts full of bats are near the door, and there's a scattering of laundry hampers, wastebaskets, and spittoons set within throwing (or spitting) distance of the lockers.

And that's it. The only hint of luxury is the huge television screen dominating the players' lounge—a space about the size of a middle-class suburban living room located to the rear right of the clubhouse —and that hint is somewhat offset by the comfortable but unquestionably institutional couches that furnish the lounge.

Except for the plastic name tag each bears, the lockers are virtually indistinguishable. They are the same size, have pretty much the same equipment, and—because the clubhouse attendants distribute fresh ones before every game—even have the uniforms hung in the same place. These arrangements reflect the time-honored and thoroughly romantic belief that all Yankees are created equal.

To the right as one walks in, after a handful of lockers used by assistant coaches and late arrivals who come up from the minors after the major league rosters expand on September 1, there's a gaggle of pitchers: Jay Howell, Shane Rawley, and around the corner, Dave Righetti and Ron Guidry. Between them, in a corner locker that's just large enough to accommodate his folding beach chair and keep him

< x >

well out of the clubhouse traffic patterns, is the Yankee captain, Graig Nettles.

The lockers between Guidry's and the corridor leading to the manager's office belong to coaches Roy White, Don Zimmer, and Yogi Berra; just beyond the corridor is one that started out the season as Art Fowler's and wound up as Lee Walls's. Next to Walls's comes another row of pitchers, including the only two lockers that may be said to be decorated: Goose Gossage's and Rudy May's. The decoration in each case consists of a single picture torn from a magazine and taped over the locker entrance. May has what appears to be a New Guinea native playing a primitive flute; Gossage, a wooded landscape. Beyond them, on the way to the players' lounge, is a more or less "official" bulletin board carrying notices from the American League, memos from George Steinbrenner, and the occasional spectacularly witty or obscene fan letter.

The back wall is given over mostly to catchers, outfielders, and the young Yankee staff who do double duty as batting-practice pitchers and catchers and who operate the computer, speed gun, and videotape during the game. At its left extreme, just before the entrance to the trainer's room, are lockers for trainer Gene Monahan and his assistant. Jerry Mumphrey began his season back there, but finished it 1500 miles away, in Houston.

The lockers flanking the entrance to the shower along the left-hand wall also saw some comings and goings during the year. The most dramatic occurred early in the season, when Bobby Murcer's rocking chair was retired, along with Murcer. John Montefusco, Omar Moreno, Ray Fontenot, and Larry Milbourne were that wall's added occupants—Montefusco and Milbourne joining Ken Griffey, Dave Winfield, Don Baylor, and Thurman Munson's still-empty locker in the area beyond the showers, Moreno and Fontenot joining Willie Randolph and Roy Smalley nearer the front door.

But even if the Yankee roster had remained constant during the year, the relative starkness and simplicity of the locker room insists not only on equality but on interchangeability—finally, on expendability. Compared to the space afforded even the most long-term Yankee player, the manager's office supplies at least the architecture of stability. Located down a corridor to the right of the locker room, it's about the size of the players' lounge but has none of that room's

< xi >

institutional aura. For 1983, at least, it bore the stamp of Billy Martin.

It's dominated by a large, dark executive desk whose surface is often cluttered with the manager's correspondence. There are always a couple of pipes at hand, and a tobacco humidor. The wood-paneled walls are liberally hung with Martin memorabilia—a photo of him with Willie Nelson, an early cover of *Sport* magazine dating from his playing days, a more recent one from *Sports Illustrated* labelling him "The Yankee's Fiery Genius," a letter from Ronald Reagan, and—behind the manager's chair—a framed uniform jersey and photomontage of his idol, Casey Stengel.

There are couches and chairs along the walls, but they're at a safe distance from the desk. The manager is separated from them not only by the desk itself but also by an open space wide enough to accommodate the twenty or so reporters who appear after each game. Perhaps most important, the manager's office has privacy: his own shower and toilet, his own refrigerator, and a door that shuts. One enters the manager's office by invitation only.

To a degree, the clubhouse reflects the way power is distributed within the Yankee organization, and one could be forgiven for imagining that the man in the wood-paneled office, whoever he might be, exercised absolute control over the players. But for all the differences between them, the players and the manager are all in the basement; the owner is upstairs, where the paneling is darker, the carpet deeper. Of the two phones on the manager's desk, one connects directly with those Yankee offices. Perhaps more in 1983 than in any other recent year, the Yankees were the manager's team, but finally they—and the manager—were employees of George M. Steinbrenner III.

This book, a product of a season spent with the Yankees—at home and on the road, from spring's optimism to autumn's despair—is about the ways the diamond, the clubhouse, and the executive suite come together to shape a baseball team. It doesn't pretend to any vast backlog of baseball expertise—it's written by a sometimes passionate but more often casual fan—but for the last decade or so I've made my living by watching and listening, and in seven months of that, you can learn a lot.

The Yankees, virtually all of them, helped. Dale Murray must have alternated two different pitching motions twenty times for me before I suddenly saw, with blinding and unforgettable clarity, the difference

< xii >

in his center of weight; Lou Piniella, after he made me prove that it was indeed possible to talk in lay terms about the proper way to hit a *tennis* ball, was a patient lecturer on the art and craft of batting. Almost every other coach and player—sometimes late at night in the bar, sometimes in a quiet corner of the locker room—taught me something about the game, about themselves. Those late-night conversations, when my notebook was tucked away in my pocket, were by tacit agreement off the record; though I transcribed them as accurately as I could when I returned to my room, I have honored that understanding. But they inform every page of this book, and I am grateful.

Because I kept learning all through the season, I've used hindsight liberally. The chapters are organized roughly according to chronology, but I've nowhere pretended to an innocence—or to a belief that the Yankees might win their division—that was no longer mine by the season's end. I've let the first chapter stand pretty much as it was written for the *Village Voice,* and it can serve as a first-impression benchmark; but the other sections that draw on *Voice* articles have been revised, often heavily.

I'm grateful to the *Voice*'s editor, David Schneiderman, for freeing me from my other responsibilities so that I could spend seven months on this project; it was he who had the idea that I should go down to Florida and take a look at the Yankees. Ted Solotaroff, at Harper & Row, first had the notion that my Yankee-watching might yield a book; he deserves praise for the courage of this idea, but no blame for its result.

Throughout the regular season, and after, the Yankee personnel entrusted with the care and metaphorical feeding of reporters were unfailingly courteous and helpful. That's their job, of course, but they did it well, and I thank them. My deepest debts and profoundest gratitude, however, are to the reporters and broadcasters who regularly covered the team. They were patient with my rookie mistakes, generous with their knowledge. And in grim places like Arlington, Texas—a "city" which to my viewpoint consisted solely of traffic cloverleafs—the traveling writers helped preserve my sanity. To them —Bill Madden and Jack Lang of the *News,* Joe Donnelly and Marty Noble of *Newsday,* Moss Klein of the *Newark Star-Ledger,* Murray Chass, Gerald Eskenazi, and Jane Gross of the *Times,* Mike McAlary

< xiii >

and Bob Klapisch of the *Post,* Dick Gutwillig of the Westchester-Rockland papers, and Claire Smith of the *Hartford Courant*—I shall always be grateful. When they appear in this book, it's because of what they wrote; when they appear in my mind, it's for what they meant to me. Baseball travel and baseball hours, especially with the Yankees, where something *always* seems to be going on, are hellish, and without their friendship, the long absences from my family would have been nearly unendurable. Thanks.

< xiv >

The 1983 Season: A Chronology

APRIL 5: Opening Day, Yankees lose to Seattle. Piniella on disabled list.

APRIL 13: Roger Erickson sent down to Columbus.

APRIL 15: Martin ejected for disputing strike calls, fined $5,000.

APRIL 18: Erickson suspended for failure to report to Columbus.

APRIL 19: Steinbrenner fined $50,000 for spring-training tirade against National League umpires.

APRIL 22: Piniella activated.

APRIL 29: Martin ejected from game in Texas, kicks dirt at umpires, draws suspension.

APRIL 30: Steinbrenner in Texas for meetings with Martin and players; Cerone scratched from starting lineup. Randolph returned to New York for medical examination of knee.

MAY 4: Campaneris activated, Mattingly sent to Columbus. Erickson pitches for Columbus.

MAY 6: Gossage finally gets first save of season.

MAY 10: Wynegar injures arm in plate collision; goes on disabled list, 5/13.

MAY 15: Martin confronts Henry Hecht in Yankee clubhouse.

MAY 24: Martin in barroom scuffle in Anaheim.

< xv >

MAY 27: Wynegar reactivated. Winfield ejected for shoving Oakland catcher after brushback, flurry of Steinbrenner press releases follows.

MAY 31: Doyle Alexander (0–7) designated for reassignment, Balboni activated.

JUNE 1: Steinbrenner suspended for May 27 actions.

JUNE 9: "Mandatory" workout in Milwaukee turns out to be voluntary.

JUNE 15: Matt Keough acquired from Oakland for two minor leaguers. Martin and Steinbrenner meet in Cleveland, Martin's future unresolved.

JUNE 16: Balboni optioned to Columbus.

JUNE 17: Art Fowler removed as pitching coach by Steinbrenner; Martin throws *New York Times* researcher out of clubhouse.

JUNE 19: Rudy May on 21-day disabled list with back injury; Ray Fontenot called up from minors.

JUNE 20: Murcer "retires," Mattingly reactivated.

JUNE 21: American League report clears Martin in June 17 incident.

JUNE 27: Randolph on disabled list; Barry Evans called up from Columbus, refuses to report.

JUNE 29: Meacham called up, Evans designated for reassignment.

JUNE 30: Murray Cook named Yankee general manager.

JULY 4: Righetti pitches no-hitter; Yankees 12–5 since June 15.

JULY 12: Randolph reactivated, Meacham returned to minors.

JULY 14: Yankees turn fourteenth error in last six games.

JULY 16: Randolph on disabled list again. Milbourne purchased from Phillies.

JULY 17: Griffey disabled, Balboni brought up.

JULY 24: Pine-tar game.

JULY 27: Yankees complete Texas sweep, for twelfth win in last thirteen games, take share of first place for first time since April 16, 1982.

JULY 28: Pine-tar victory overturned, Yankees fall from first.

JULY 31: Martin ejected, calls umpire Dale Ford a "stone liar" during postgame interview.

AUGUST 2: Griffey reactivated, Balboni sent down.

AUGUST 4: Winfield kills sea gull with warm-up throw, is arrested.

AUGUST 7: Jay Howell has knee surgery.

< xvi >

AUGUST 10: Randolph reactivated, Milbourne refuses reassignment to Columbus. Campaneris is conveniently disabled.

AUGUST 10: Jerry Mumphrey traded to Houston for Omar Moreno. Martin hears news on phone, responds, "Oh, shit."

AUGUST 16: Piniella comes out of ballgame ill.

AUGUST 18: Robertson injured in car crash. Pine-tar game completed, Yankees lose.

AUGUST 26: John Montefusco obtained from San Diego for two minor leaguers.

SEPTEMBER 2–3: Martin serves suspension for July 31 incident.

SEPTEMBER 8: Kemp injured by batted ball during pregame practice, hospitalized.

SEPTEMBER 9: Yankees, in undisputed possession of second place after 9–4 road trip, face league-leading Baltimore in four-game series at Stadium. Win opener on Nettles's homer, close to four games behind.

SEPTEMBER 10–11: Baltimore sweeps remaining games, virtually eliminating Yankees.

SEPTEMBER 16: Another round of "Martin fired" stories.

SEPTEMBER 25: Yankees mathematically eliminated.

SEPTEMBER 29: Dale Ford, citing "great pain, suffering, and mental anguish," sues Martin for slander.

OCTOBER 2: Season ends, Yankees (91–71) in third place.

< xvii >

1

The Paranoid Style in Yankee Baseball

It is about 10 o'clock in the morning, the Florida sun is already heating up, and I am standing outside a closed gate at the New York Yankees' Fort Lauderdale training camp. I give the security man my name and tell him I have an appointment with the Yankees' PR director, Ken Nigro. The guard does not move. It is clear to him that I'm trying to pull some kind of fast one. I reach into my pocket to produce the working-press card issued by the New York City Police Department. My picture is on it. In color.

The guard reaches two fingers through the fence for the card. He looks several times at it, several times at me, but he does not open the gate. Neither does he return the card. Carrying it with him, he walks the fifteen yards to the press trailer. A moment or two later, he emerges, opens the gate just barely wide enough to admit me, and hands back the card. "They're expecting you," he says. He sounds disappointed.

Waiting inside the trailer, already typed out on the reception desk, is the little pink pass that will admit me to the field, clubhouse, press box, etc., for the duration of spring training. Nigro is there too. Tall, whippet-thin, and with a haircut that could pass for punk if it wasn't vaguely military, he takes two rapid steps backward as I enter his

< 1 >

office. Eventually he recovers and shakes my hand almost as though he didn't believe it carried a communicable disease. We talk politely for a minute or two, and I ask him for a media guide. Though these pocket-sized fact books were once, years ago, more or less internal documents distributed only to the media and other baseball clubs, most teams now print them up by the tens of thousands and sell them as souvenirs. The Yankees' costs five bucks at the Stadium, six by mail. Nigro hesitates, finally unhasps a trunk near the door, and removes one. "You're *very* lucky," he says, "we have only a few left."

I thank him, consider offering to shake his hand again but decide that I don't want to unnerve him, and start to leave the office. "One thing," he says, "just a word of advice."

"Yes?"

"You're interested in Billy Martin, right?"

"Yes."

"I wouldn't ask him any questions if I were you. He can be, er, *difficult.*"

It is a truism of administrative theory that the speed of change in any organization is inversely related to the organization's complexity. When Jimmy Carter wanted to send peanuts to market, they went; when he tried to counter Pentagon procedures, nothing happened. Major league baseball clubs—front offices, farm teams, scouts, players, coaches, agents, broadcast subsidiaries, union reps—are relatively complex entities; though the advent of free agency made it possible to work significant year-to-year changes in the players' roster, *organizational* character yielded only grudgingly. Even in the darkest days of the Horace Clarke era, the Yankees' off-field personality was as patrician and imperial as it had been in their days of greatness. The imperialism remains to some degree (in most spring training camps, security consists of a retiree tilted back in a folding chair), but the essential hallmark of the Yankees has changed in the decade since George Steinbrenner purchased the club in 1973. By now, at every level in the organization—from the guard at the gate to the principal owner in his private box—the Yankees are marked by a broad streak of paranoia.

Before getting into definitions, I should point out that it is not necessarily a bad thing for an organization to exhibit symptoms of

< 2 >

paranoia. Within the United States government, for instance, there are several thriving bureaucracies that are *supposed* to be obsessed with the notion that someone—the Russians, the Cubans, the Yippies —is out to get us. That is their job, and as long as some countervailing force keeps their twitching fingers off the launch button, it may even be a useful one. Paranoia becomes dangerous or self-defeating only when it achieves the kind of dominance it has with the Yankees.

Clinically, paranoia can be defined as a malfunction marked by systematized delusions of grandeur ("I am the pope.") or of persecution ("The media are out to get me."). Authorities generally recognize that, except in a schizophrenic state, the disorder can coexist with an otherwise intact mental and psychological condition. Paranoia *can* involve hallucinations ("See that short man in the lavender suit over there? *He's* one of them."), but as a garden-variety neurosis, it involves problems of interpreting reality, not of perceiving it.

Thus, on the afternoon of March 25, when the Yankees were trailing the Expos 5–2 in the bottom of the eighth, approximately 7,000 observers were in general agreement that Roy Smalley's leadoff line drive to right field was perhaps trapped, rather than caught, by the Montreal outfielder. The umpire thought not, however, and as Smalley chugged into second with an apparent double, he signaled that the ball had been caught. George Steinbrenner, standing surrounded by reporters in an area along the right-field line near the Yankee clubhouse, disagreed. "Schmuck," he shouted (registering unhappiness, disappointment, and grief). Then, as reporters dutifully transcribed his words, he continued, "This happens every spring. The damn National League umps are all homers. [NL president Chub] Feeney tells them to give close calls to the National League teams" (thereby registering paranoid belief in a conspiracy).

Steinbrenner's charge, being news, was duly reported, and as might be expected, caused some raised eyebrows in the commissioner's office. Steinbrenner responded neither with a denial nor with an apology but by promptly banning all reporters from the area in which he'd been standing (thereby positing Conspiracy B). The ban, creating the George Steinbrenner memorial zone of silence, was enforced by two uniformed Fort Lauderdale police. Throughout the remaining home games, though Steinbrenner never deigned to enter the quarantined area himself, he periodically craned forward from the

< 3 >

owner's box to make sure that it was clear of reporters.

There are a couple of points to be made here. First, paranoia is an *organizing* principle, imposing order (the umps are out to get me) on chance (working with only a three-man crew, they blew the call). To invent, and reinvent on the spot, an explanation for *every* event, which leaves one never at fault, always a victim, is hard work and demands a creative intelligence. It is, for instance, just barely imaginable that Feeney told his umps to be biased—though it is hardly likely he would think this the ideal way to get them ready for the National League season.

Second, the existence of real power makes it considerably easier to sustain one's paranoid delusions. For openers, Steinbrenner indicted the reporters as co-conspirators in the attempt to embarrass him, and then, by banning them from the area in which they'd been watching late innings ever since the Yankees moved to Lauderdale, in 1962, he *proved* they were part of it (see Richard Nixon, Daniel Ellsberg, and "national security"). Otherwise, he'd have let them stay there, right? He's a rational guy.

When things aren't going as he demands, Steinbrenner vents his feelings of betrayal by scattershot attacks, often vilifying the players he's spent millions on. His impulsive—and ultimately reversed—1973 decision to trade away Bobby Murcer after a pop-up was an early example; his repeated remarks in 1982 that Winfield wasn't a "winner" like Reggie indicate that he hasn't changed much. Indeed, during 1982's rotating circus of managers and pitching coaches, the Yankee clubhouse was often as sullen and suspicious as the principal owner himself. Long before they became a fifth-place team, the Yankees had started acting like one.

This spring—only partly, I think, because it *was* spring—the team seemed more relaxed. A slumping Cerone could work on his stance with Piniella, and Murcer could terrify a hungover player with the spurious news that he'd be dh-ing during the afternoon's game. Winfield seemed particularly at ease and secure in his role as the team's on-field leader. "A lot of it," he said, "is that Billy protects us from George. Not in any direct sense, maybe—though I think he'll do that too, if he has to—but that he acts as a lightning rod." Winfield broke off to guffaw as another player, reacting to the deaths in the Lippizanner stables, shouted across the room to the trainer's office, "Hey,

< 4 >

Gene. If that stuff kills horses, how come it only makes Willie's lip sore?" Then he continued: "This year when George wants to scream at someone, he'll scream at Billy and just let us play baseball."

Billy Martin, the likely target for Steinbrenner's predictable rages, has been a favorite victim of authority for much of his life; after the famous Copacabana incident in 1957, you can be sure it wasn't Ford or Mantle, the other two participants, whom the Yankees traded. Now nearing the age of fifty-five, he has all of Steinbrenner's intelligence and eye for conspiracy, but only he (occasionally) believes he has Steinbrenner's power. Martin is often fond of pointing out to his players and to reporters that he's both "a man and a manager." As a man, he manifests all the characteristics of negative paranoia—every fight he ever got into was the other guy's fault; every baseball job he's ever lost was because people poisoned the owner against him—but as a manager, he makes the paranoid mindset work for him.

The concept of "positive paranoia" was first discussed by Andrew Weil in his 1974 book *The Natural Mind.* Weil argued that paranoia, usually treated as a unitary phenomenon, actually had two parts: first, the imposition or discovery of a pattern in random events, and second, the interpretation of that pattern as hostile. Citing work done at San Francisco's Mt. Zion Hospital during the Haight-Ashbury heyday, Weil noted the existence of a significant number of people who exhibited the typical paranoid's obsessive drive to explain every single blot in even the most complex Rorschach test but who appeared to believe, quite happily, "that the universe is a conspiracy organized for their own benefit." In sports, such a tendency is called "a winning attitude."

To watch a Billy Martin training camp is to discover the positive side of paranoia at work. To the occasional observer, baseball often appears a collection of random events—hit a round, spinning ball with a round bat and who knows where the damn thing will go?—but winning teams win precisely because they can impose a pattern on that randomness. Offensively, they hit behind the runner or execute the squeeze; defensively, they have a coordinated, routine response for virtually every situation. There is no predicting, for instance, the precise way a bunt attempting to move a runner from first to second will roll, but the defensive response—the first and third basemen charging, the second baseman covering first, the shortstop covering

< 5 >

second, the left fielder breaking toward third—is designed to incorporate the random roll of the ball into a pattern determined by the team in the field.

To create such patterns, to imagine and neutralize virtually anything an offensive team can do, is to exercise positive paranoia; and Martin's teams practice these routines endlessly and inventively: runners on first and third, no out, and the batter pops a foul near the stands behind first base. What is the play?

The intuitive play, of course, is for the first or second baseman, whoever catches the ball, to heave it home and prevent a run from scoring. The problem is that a throw from short right field to home may be wasted if the runner on third is only bluffing, and will allow anyone but Rusty Staub to tag up and go from first to second, thus putting two runners in scoring position and eliminating the prospect of a routine double play. Most clubs defense the pop foul, then, by having the pitcher run to a spot on the direct line between where the foul is caught and home plate and act as cutoff man. Martin, instead, has the pitcher break straight for first base, and drills his fielders to fire the ball directly to the inside corner of the base. This pins the runner on first, obviously, but it also eliminates the prospect of a direct throw home. Does it work?

Coach Don Zimmer is positioned near the boxes behind first, tossing pops into the air and letting either Don Baylor or Willie Randolph call for the ball. As he tosses it, Bob Shirley races from the pitcher's mound to first base. At the precise moment the ball is caught, Jerry Mumphrey, perhaps the fastest Yankee regular, tags up at third and tries to score. Time after time, Shirley's relay to the catcher nips him. The drill, with different runners, fielders, and pitchers, goes on for almost twenty minutes.

"You set up the play that way," says Martin later, "to make their first-base coach play defense for you, and you practice it with a fast runner on third to convince everyone it'll work. If a player not only knows *what* to do, but believes it's what he *should* be doing, he's gonna do it right ninety-nine times out of a hundred. On a play like that, if anyone stops to think—Willie, the pitcher—the runner scores, so you drill and make it as routine as the pitcher covering first on a grounder."

How often during the course of a season does the situation they just

< 6 >

practiced come up? "Maybe only three or four times a year," he says, "but maybe a dozen or so. Maybe three times in one *game*. But even if it's only once, you fuckin' well better be ready for it."

Martin, pretty much an autodidact since high school, is a Civil War buff, and military thinking is the paradigm of positive paranoia. Conceive a strategy, devise tactics, drill, and execute. And, of course, the enemy *is* out to get you.

In baseball, the other team is out to win, so field generalship is an appropriate mode. Roy Smalley, nine years in baseball and going through his first full spring with Martin, talked about the system: "There's more money here, first of all, which means more coaches to work with you, which means more time actually to *practice,* instead of just taking infield or bp. There's an attention to detail here that I've never seen anywhere else, except maybe a little with Gene Mauch.

"But I think Billy's real genius as a manager is that he knows what to do with a *particular* team. At Oakland, he had to steal every run he could get, so he invented Billy Ball—you guys named it that, he didn't. But with this lineup, he can afford to wait for the big inning, so he'll be more conservative, stealing a run only when he has to, or just enough to keep the other guys off balance. I mean, even though we're loaded with power, he's made damn sure that *everyone* knows how to squeeze."

The threat works for him. Leading the Dodgers 1–0 in the seventh inning of a game at Vero Beach, the Yankees load the bases off Fernando Valenzuela on a single, an error, and a walk. With the bottom three hitters coming up, everyone in the park is thinking Billy Ball, and the corners move in onto the grass and toward the foul lines. But Andre Robertson swings away and lines a single to right through the hole where the first baseman might have been. The corners move back as Otis Nixon comes up swinging. He tops a ball toward third, and Valenzuela has to field it, too late for a play. With pitcher Shane Rawley, who may not lift a bat again all year, in the box, the infield moves in again. But even Rawley swings, sending a grounder neatly through the too wide gap between third and short. By the time the inning is over, the Yankees lead 8–0.

After the game, Martin laughed about the sequence. "That's what you call Billy Bull, right? If they know you can execute the squeeze —and if they know you're *willing* to do it—they've got to defense it.

< 7 >

As soon as they do, they give you a bunch of other options."

Though Martin's Yankees will often be able to wait for their power to carry them, they will probably not be staid. Throughout the spring, they worked on a complicated decoy double steal involving the runner on first apparently slipping as he breaks for second, and drawing a throw that would let a runner on third come home. It is perhaps a little *too* tricky, and after a game against the Expos during which Nettles ran directly into the waiting arms of the Montreal catcher, Martin was testy. "*Nettles* worked it right," he insisted. "Mumphrey just got a little too far off base."

But what was supposed to happen?

"Listen, it's supposed to be a surprise play. How can it be a fuckin' surprise if you put it in the paper?"

Martin's attitude toward the press is complex. He is extremely sensitive to the fact that writers can be his allies—tacitly agreeing that certain things are "automatically" off the record—and he cultivates the beat reporters assiduously. As spring training wound down, for instance, everyone was involved in the who'll-make-the-team guessing game; Martin leaked the final roster to the regular reporters twenty-four hours before it was officially released. He was able to do this, of course, partly because he knew them and trusted them enough to know that one of them wouldn't rush up to Butch Hobson while he was still hoping to make the team and ask how it felt to be cut. In that sense, it's easy to explain the way Martin works with the regular writers, but nothing (except, perhaps, suppressed resentment that he *does* have to be nice to the major dailies) can quite explain the occasional cruelty he shows to other journalists. An hour or so before a Lauderdale game against the Astros, Martin was sitting in the dugout talking with me and a *Newsday* reporter when a puppy-dog of a kid bounced up. "Excuse me, Mr. Martin," he said, "I'm with the Pace College newspaper, can I ask you a few questions?"

"Sure, sit right down here next to me and ask away."

The kid got his tape recorder working and began with the obvious roster question. "I'm going to tell all the writers that at the same time," Martin said. The kid tried to rephrase it. "Didn't I just tell you I was going to tell all the writers that at the same time?" Flustered, and without the experience to slide to another subject, the kid sort of burbled about how many pitchers the Yankees might carry. Martin

< 8 >

looked at him as though he was dogshit: "If I answer that, it'll make three times I've told you the same thing. Twice is enough, isn't it?" His ears red with embarrassment, the kid shut off his recorder and got up. "Right, thanks, Mr. Martin. Have a good year." "Sure, same to you. . . ." And as the kid walked away, he continued, " . . . asshole."

Logically, Martin was right. A half-dozen reporters had been working for a month to figure out the answer to those questions, and he was hardly going to stiff them and give it to a kid on a day pass, but the combative, bullying nature of his response was surely not a matter of logic. When things are not going as he wants—when they aren't fitting the pattern he's designed—Martin can be weirdly short-fused.

Still, though I don't believe that someone else started *every* fight he ever got into (and if you believe Martin's explanation that he offered to bet the famous marshmallow salesman three hundred dollars to a penny that he could kick the salesman's ass in order to *avoid* a fight by making the salesman leave him alone, I hope the Easter Bunny brings you lots of candy), it's clear that Martin's rep has made him something of a target. A Fort Myers cop who was on crowd-control duty when Martin arrived for spring's final game said, "At first I didn't recognize him. He was wearing a cowboy hat and had an attractive young woman in the car with him, but he made a couple of jokes and seemed in a real good mood. When he got out of the car, he was signing autographs for all the kids and laughing. But out of nowhere, this one guy—a pretty big guy—started shoving him and shouting at him. Martin shoved him back once—not hard, just to get him away—and I had to grab the guy and lead him off." If the cop hadn't been there, headlines again.

In general, most of the players appreciate Martin's readiness for at least a metaphorical fight. Bob Shirley, who came to the Yankees as a free agent during the off-season, would feel differently once he'd been dropped from the starting rotation after a single bad outing, but in Lauderdale he was full of praise for Martin. "I'm really looking forward to playing for him. San Diego, and especially Cincinnati last year, it was almost like nobody cared what happened. You win, you lose, you get a bad call . . . so what. Billy's different. *He* wants to win, he wants *you* to win, and you know that if anything goes wrong, he's a hundred percent on your side. You know the fielders are going to be making the plays, too, because *they* know how much he wants

< 9 >

to win. Everything is going to be different this year."

Well, yes and no. There is no questioning Martin's will to win—barely able to stand up straight after an attack of food poisoning that struck down fifteen Yankees after their New Orleans road trip, Martin managed to lurch up from the trainer's table and chew out Rudy May for having walked six and hit one batter during less than an inning of a B-squad game—but there are limits to willpower. Despite their strong spring, the Yankees' starting rotation remains shaky, and Baltimore has to be the division favorite. Belief can carry a galvanized team of college kids through a short tournament, but it's unlikely to sustain professional athletes over a 162-game season; they know too much.

And like all neuroses, paranoia—whether positive or negative—exists because it serves the function of making reality easier for the neurotic to deal with. The intellectual struggle involved in fitting external events into a preconceived pattern pays off by providing a coherence that lets the paranoid function with consistency—and often with brilliance. Over time, however, not even the most fertile imagination can keep pace with life's curveballs; at that point, either the systematization stretches so far that it tips over into a psychotic creation of unreality, or the paranoid is forced to abandon it, often sinking into deep depression. Given good breaks, Martin may be able to sustain his positive paranoia over an entire season, but it seems inevitably to crumble with time. As Maury Allen wrote in his 1980 bio, *Damn Yankee,* "The scouting report on Martin said he would have one personality for the first year of his managerial career and another—uglier, meaner, and more sarcastic—later. He would play to the press in his first season, buddy up with the players, drinking socially and laughing with them about common enemies, the press and management, and charm the fans. Things would change later as his own insecurities would surface, his own ego would take hold, his true nature would spring to the fore."

The difference between the '81 and '82 seasons with Oakland provides the most recent demonstration that Allen was right about the superficial pattern, but he's wrong to suggest that the ugly Martin is somehow truer to nature than Billy the Good. The natures are one and the same; it is external events that determine which dominates. All the things which have made Martin the best dugout manager in

< 10 >

the game, year in and year out, contribute to his apparently inescapable loss of control. Every game in which Martin and his teams are able to control chance within the boundaries of the playing field leaves him more vulnerable to the breakdown when off-field events remind him how little control he really has.

Injuries, throughout his managerial career, have driven Martin round the bend. Prior to the famous "One's a born liar, the other's convicted" remark that led to his first departure from the Yankees in 1978, Martin had been trying to buy time with a jury-rigged team. Three starting pitchers (Hunter, Messersmith, Gullett) and his best long reliever (Tidrow) couldn't throw. His double-play combination (Dent and Randolph) was out, center fielder Mickey Rivers fractured his hand, and catcher Thurman Munson was so crippled by cysts it pained him even to squat behind the plate. The same ability to see patterns that makes Martin a great manager began to give him the creepy crawlies. The only explanation for all these events was a more sinister kind of pattern. It was Reggie's fault, or George's, or even Henry Hecht's. Or maybe, in an unholy conspiracy, all three of them: "The press made it so much harder for all of us," Martin has written. "Henry Hecht of the *New York Post* was the worst, . . . he'd try to pit player against player, or a player against me, or me against George. He'd do that all the time." Eventually, preoccupied by the plotting he *knew* was going on in the clubhouse and the front office, Martin lost his grip on what was happening on the ballfield. He begin issuing confusing instructions to the bullpen, at one point telling Sparky Lyle to get up and soft-toss and a minute later calling to find out if he was ready to go into the game.

In another setting—one where the owner wasn't already preoccupied by his belief that the manager, the press, and the players were part of the conspiracy operating against *him*—it is possible that Martin could survive his various crises. He didn't make it through Oakland's sore-armed 1982, it's true, but one can at least imagine a setting in which he could simply hold on for a while, then gradually recover. That situation does not exist with George Steinbrenner's Yankees.

< 11 >

2

Who's on First and Who's at Short and Third and in Right . . . ?

There are dozens of different jobs to be done during spring training: plays to be learned, mechanics practiced, swings grooved, tired muscles unkinked . . . but the manager has one primary job. He has to decide who's going to play for him, and where.

Once upon a time, at least according to baseball nostalgiasts and historians, the job was fairly straightforward. Except for the occasional trade, the same players were in the organization year after year. Once in a while, a rookie might squeeze a veteran out; sometimes, a vet would drink himself off the team. But since free agency, and especially with a club that has taken advantage of the new rules with the reckless enthusiasm of the Yankees, roster decisions have grown more complicated.

During the off-season, for instance, the Yankees acquired Don Baylor as a free agent. A decade earlier, getting a player of Baylor's proven ability would probably have required a trade, which would have made room for him on the twenty-five-man roster major league teams are permitted to carry. Here was Baylor, however, with a guaranteed contract which essentially insured him the designated

< 12 >

hitter's spot in the lineup, and here were not one, not two, but three people who used to fill that spot—and who together, as it happens, filled it last year at least as well as Baylor had for the California Angels. Here are Baylor's 1982 batting stats, most of which were as dh, measured against the figures compiled by the Yankees' Piniella, Gamble, and (occasionally) Murcer combo.

	AVG	G	AB	R	H	2B	3B	HR	RBI	BB	SO	SB
Baylor	.263	157	608	80	160	24	1	24	93	57	69	10
Yankee dh's	.275	162	625	67	172	31	1	28	109	63	81	7

If you now have four people where there's really a place for only one, what are you going to do? You can try to trade a superfluous player, but that too is not as easy as it used to be. Certain players have no-trade clauses in their contracts, and virtually every Yankee of even marginal desirability has a salary so bloated that other clubs may be unwilling to assume it. This is especially true in cases where players —like, as it happens, the three Yankee dh's—are either aging or nearing free agency, or both.

As a small exercise in understanding how difficult the job facing Martin at the start of the 1983 season actually was, put yourself in his mind for a few pages. Consider the internal politics—the long-standing friendships and loyalties—of your team. Consider the *pride* of professional ballplayers, how much each one of them wants to earn his money. Consider, too, that it is March 25, a week before the start of the season, and most teams are already down to twenty-eight or twenty-nine players, well within grasp of the twenty-five-man limit. In your camp, there are still forty players, and the ubiquitous crew of New York writers is starting to make jokes about "Martinomics" as a solution to the nation's unemployment problem. Let's begin with your taking a look at the ripples spreading out from the Baylor acquisition.

Well, if you have to make Baylor dh, you could always platoon Piniella and Gamble in right field. Or at least you could have until the Yankees acquired Steve Kemp, an everyday right fielder, through free agency. That means that your problem isn't fitting four players

< 13 >

into two slots, which was bad enough, but five. Maybe, since Piniella and Gamble can't play center, you could move Winfield over from left, at once getting rid of the outfield's weak defensive link, Jerry Mumphrey, and opening up a spot so you can both get the Gamble/-Piniella bat into the lineup on a regular basis and (as an important side-effect on team morale) keep two club leaders happy. Sounds good, right?

Yes. To everyone but Winfield. At thirty-one, though he's still a superlative athlete capable of handling Yankee Stadium's huge center field, he doesn't think he can play it every day. He's convinced, and there are at least some knowledgeable people who think he's right, that the daily grind of covering 50 percent more territory would affect him at the plate and on the bases. The shape and size of his body—at six feet six inches by no means a typical baseball player's—put tremendous pressure on his knees, so this judgment is plausible. But even if he's wrong, it doesn't matter; as long as he *believes* he's right, you've got a self-fulfilling prophecy in the classic mode. Are you going to risk screwing up Dave Winfield in order to get Oscar Gamble some playing time? Hardly.

All right, then, you have to forget about trades, and forget about finding a regular spot for any of last year's dh's (except maybe for Oscar if Baylor has trouble hitting right-handers—he never has, but this might be the year; you could try prayer). You'll just have to bite the bullet and release one of them. Who's the most expendable? Murcer, by a long shot.

This, in fact, was on the front office's mind long before you were rehired, and Murcer came to camp without a major league contract. Technically, he's signed to the Yankees' Triple-A team at Columbus, and if you have to release someone, he's the likely candidate. He's popular with the fans—though maybe not as popular as Piniella—but that problem can be handled. In fact, it already has been: there's a job in the Yankee broadcast booth waiting for him.

The trouble with that is that Murcer shows no sign of wanting to begin his television career quite yet. In what has to be counted as one of the all-time great displays of pressure hitting—his annual player contract of $375,000 is squarely on the line—Murcer comes to camp and hits the bejeezus out of the ball. In his first three games, he goes 4-for-4, with two ribbies. Besides, you want him in your clubhouse.

< 14 >

Not just because he's potentially a good influence but because he likes you, and when the inevitable midseason confrontation with George comes around it would be nice to have an established player singing your praises. Even if you weren't morbidly aware of conspiracies afoot against you, you'd have to know that there are a few players in there who don't think you're nearly as wonderful as your press clippings. And speaking of those guys, why on earth are you giving Ken Griffey so much playing time in right field. Didn't you tell him he was going to be your first baseman?

You did, but you've also got two—and maybe three—other guys who can play first. Steve Balboni has led the International League in home runs for the last three seasons, and George thinks he deserves a chance at the Stadium. You know that Death Valley, the Stadium's swollen left field, is going to turn a lot of those minor league homers into major league outs, but you've got at least to appear to be giving the kid a chance. One thing George knows for sure is that home run hitters—especially white, Italian home run hitters—can fill a lot of seats. You, however, are less concerned with Balboni than with Roy Smalley. In a lot of ways, Smalley is your kind of player. He's aggressive, gets about as much out of himself as there is to get, thinks well, and bats in some runs. For this you would be willing to overlook one of his bad habits (he reads hardcover books) and live with his limited range at shortstop. But he may not be able to play short for you, because there's this kid Andre Robertson who's already the best defensive shortstop on the club—and maybe in the division—and George is already raving about him to the press. Unless Robertson proves totally unable to hit major league pitching (something that is certainly possible), you may *have* to play him. Which means you've got to give Smalley a long look at first base.

Why not at third, a position for which he seems eminently qualified and which is not nearly as overcrowded as first? Because Graig Nettles is your third baseman for as long as he has the strength to take the field, that's why. He's as close to a friend as you have among the players, for one thing, and for another (though your belief is shared neither widely nor in the owner's box), you don't think he's washed up. For whatever reasons, you've managed to convince yourself that his recent decline at the plate (he hasn't batted above .250 or hit 20 homers since 1979) is reversible. You're going to be second-guessed

< 15 >

to death on this one, but you're standing by him.

Such loyalty is admirable, perhaps, but it's going to be awfully crowded over there at first base. Even though you've gotten rid of John Mayberry, another fading star whom George acquired, there's Don Mattingly, the player who's going to win the Dawson Award as the spring's outstanding rookie. A superlative fielder and disciplined line-drive hitter with a very good shot at batting .300, Mattingly can play the outfield, but he's primarily a first baseman.

Second base: Willie Randolph, the only easy decision in the lot. Thank God.

Things don't get a whole lot easier behind the plate. There's Rick Cerone, freshly signed to a multiyear, multidollar contract, and Butch Wynegar, who came over last year in a trade with Minnesota. Cerone, a more aggressive catcher, is very popular with the Yankee pitchers, and gives you marginally better defense. Unfortunately, he doesn't seem likely ever again to bat as well as he did in 1980, and recently has had trouble hitting right-handers at all. Wynegar represents many of the things you distrust in a player—he's quiet, unassuming, scrupulously honest—but he's a switch-hitter who's shown genuine power from both sides. At a minimum, you almost have to catch him against right-handers. Finally, there's Barry Foote, a knowledgable but aging figure who's certainly not an everyday player; Brad Gulden, not much of a hitter but an adequate third catcher; and Juan Espino, a nonroster rookie who hit .282 for Columbus last year and has been pounding the ball this spring.

First question: Do you carry two catchers or three? Given your occasional fondness for gambling, you'd like to have three. If you have only two, it's tough to pinch-hit (or pinch-run) for your starter until *very* late in the game. If you do, and your lone backup then gets hurt or tossed out in an argument, you are in deep trouble. But if you carry three with this team, you've eaten up a valuable roster spot for a guy who may get to play a dozen games if he's lucky. Maybe you have to go with two.

Okay, which two? Do you want the proven quantities, Wynegar and Cerone? If so, is Cerone—who came to camp with his head somewhat swollen by his big, long-term contract—prepared to be a platoon player? Is he further prepared to accept the fact that the lopsided ratio of right-handed starters in the league will make him the lesser part of

< 16 >

the platoon? If he won't, will the energy and aggressiveness that make you like him and regard him as a potential team leader turn him into an unbearably negative influence in the clubhouse? Since you're short on starting pitchers, do you want to trade him? Maybe you do, but he's got a no-trade contract. Besides, given Wynegar's history of injuries and illness (ten weeks on the disabled list in each of the past two seasons), do you want to run the risk of having Barry Foote or Juan Espino as your club's number-one catcher? So maybe you want to trade Wynegar. But to your practiced eye, doesn't Cerone look more and more like a guy who's going to be a lifetime .220 hitter?

At this point, even before you've begun figuring out who's going to be throwing the ball to one or more of these catchers, you understand why so many recent Yankee managers turned for occasional consolation to a bottle of Scotch. Though the players who've been putting on their pinstripes this spring are unquestionably talented individuals— as talented, if not more, than those on any other club—the 1983 Yankees are a mess. The outfield has two left fielders and two right fielders who could start on almost any team in baseball, but only one, modestly adequate, center fielder. The infield offers a choice between a shortstop who can hit, but is a second-division (though major league) fielder, and a super fielder whose lifetime major league average is .226. And when someone asks "Who's on first?" a barbershop quartet shouts "Me." And why in the world does this team have *four* designated hitters? It's as though someone took two jigsaw puzzles, jumbled them together, threw half the pieces away, and told you to put together a beautiful picture.

The imbalance becomes even more painfully obvious when you look at your pitching staff. If the rest of the team is too much of a muchness, the Yankees' starting rotation is too little of a littleness. It consists of exactly one established major league starter, and that one —left-hander Ron Guidry—may well be on the decline. He won only 14 games in 1982, and his 3.81 e.r.a., while still entirely respectable, was the highest it had been during his six seasons as a full-time major leaguer. After Guidry, only two spots in the rotation are certain: Shane Rawley, a converted reliever who started 17 games in 1982 after being traded from Seattle, and Dave Righetti, an enormously talented but erratic young left-hander who has yet to spend a full season in the majors. Query: Who is the fourth starter?

< 17 >

Indeed, since Guidry and Rawley both need four days rest between outings, who are the fourth and fifth starters? Ten-year veteran Doyle Alexander, who achieved a 1–7 record while posting a 6.08 e.r.a. after coming to the Yankees last year, isn't the hopeless case these numbers suggest, but his only truly successful seasons have come as part of a four-man rotation; the extra day of rest works against him, and he should probably be traded to a team that can get the most out of him. Unfortunately, the combination of his 1982 record and his high salary makes him virtually untradeable.

Bob Shirley, because of *his* high salary, is still another free agent who almost has to be given a starting slot. But there's even less in his record than in Alexander's to suggest he'll be much help. In only one of his six major league seasons has he compiled a winning record, and the numbers in that year (6–4 with St. Louis in 1981) are hardly the stuff of which a pennant-winning pitching staff is made.

Among younger players, there are a couple of possibilities. Roger Erickson has shown flashes of real promise during this spring, but he's coming off a sore shoulder, and there are doubts about his durability. More seriously, he's had some years of major league experience, and his lifetime record is 31–49. Still, because of that promise, he may have to stay with the team; this would be his third trip to the minors, and if he's sent down again his Yankee contract will automatically lapse, making him available, for only $25,000, to any other club that wants him. Jay Howell, another young right-hander, has shown the best stuff of any Yankee pitcher this spring. He has almost as much velocity as Gossage, as much movement on the ball as Righetti. When he's warming up in the bullpen. On the field, he's been wild, and in the six games he started for the Yankees toward the end of last season his e.r.a. was an embarrassing 7.71. But hard throwers often take a while to mature, and you certainly don't want to imitate the Mets by giving up on a pitcher who could develop the way Nolan Ryan did. Besides, Howell is also out of options, and it's far too early in his career for the organization to take a chance on losing him. He's *got* to stay; the question is: Can he be used, as regularly as Guidry, every fifth day? You're certainly not going to be able to afford 30 starts from a pitcher who gives up close to 8 runs a game. Is his problem in his head—does he simply need to learn more about how to pitch to major league hitters?—or his heart? Finally, there's a long shot: left-handed

< 18 >

sinkerballer Ray Fontenot. He too has looked good this spring, but his lack of experience is a little scary. Because of a 1981 arm problem, it took him three and a half seasons to move out of A-ball, and though he pitched very well indeed during his half-season in Double-A (2.17 e.r.a., 69 strikeouts and only 17 walks in 91 innings), the jump from Double-A to the major leagues is a big one. Maybe he's been impressive this spring only because most clubs haven't had a chance to get their second or third look at him. He's a real crapshoot. You may want to see what he can do in Columbus and then bring him up; he has all his options left and there's no risk that you'll lose him, no matter how well he pitches.

At any rate, though he's been used almost exclusively as a starter in the minors, you kind of have your eye on him as a relief pitcher. Right now, your bullpen is almost as unbalanced as your outfield; assuming Shirley works out as a starter, Rudy May will be the pen's only left-hander. Once he's out of the game, or if he's been used the day before, opposing managers can load their lineups with left-handers as soon as they get to your starter.

Except for that imbalance (and for May's worrisome spring wildness), the bullpen looks like the one solid part of the club. Goose Gossage shows every sign of still being an incomparable stopper, and George Frazier is a rubber-armed long man. Dale Murray, a hard-throwing sinkerballer acquired in an off-season trade, is a proven quantity who can be used either short or long, and the only real question about him is whether you can give him enough work to keep him sharp. When a sinkerball pitcher is too strong, from lack of work, his ball stays up, and the other team gets to take what amounts to extra batting practice. But at least early in the year, until the starters get their own strength built up, getting enough work for Murray shouldn't be a problem. With either Howell or Erickson giving you the necessary fifth reliever, the bull pen should be all right.

But the pitching remains troublesome in another way. Even if you send Fontenot down, keeping both Erickson and Howell means you'll be carrying eleven pitchers. And even if you go with only two catchers, your outfield glut makes eleven pitchers one too many. Added to thirteen pitchers and catchers, seven outfielders/dh's (Winfield, Mumphrey, Kemp, Piniella, Gamble, Baylor, and Murcer) come to twenty roster spots, leaving you only five infield places. With Smalley

< 19 >

among them, you've got some flexibility, because he can play third, short, and first. But five still isn't enough. There are going to be at least a half-dozen times during the year when one of those five will be unavailable for a game or two—flu, a death in the family, an injury too minor to take the player off the roster for the fifteen-day minimum —and it's lunacy to start a game without a single spare infielder on the bench. In addition to Robertson, who can play either second or short, you've got two possible spares still in camp. Butch Hobson is past his prime (and even during it, he had a scatter-gun arm), but he's still a respected power hitter; Bert Campaneris is past his prime by an even greater margin (he admits to being forty-one and may, in the mode of Luis Tiant, be five years older), but he still has decent speed and is a very dependable fielder. Stamina may be a real issue with him.

There's another issue as well. Campaneris had descended to the Mexican League before you brought him to camp, and the Yankees can release him without much financial pain. But Hobson is the proud possessor of a contract paying $275,000 a year. Is George going to accept paying Hobson that kind of money to play at Columbus? He's already eaten a half-million dollars worth of John Mayberry's contract; isn't that about as much as you can expect?

Now that you're glad you're not Billy Martin, let's have a word about how this mess came to be. George M. Steinbrenner III is how it came to be, and while he's among the less attractive humans in baseball, a number of people have gone broke underestimating his intelligence. When Steinbrenner took over the Yankees after the 1972 season, the franchise was a disaster area. Playing a brand of baseball that could most charitably be described as mediocre (79–76, a distant fourth place), that year's Yankees drew less than a million people for the first time since 1945. Two seasons later, they were respectable (89–73), and two seasons after that, in 1976, they won their division. Over the next five years, they finished first in their division four times, and won two World Series. Not incidentally, their attendance broke two million in every year but the strike-shortened 1981. They were winners, they were profitable, and Steinbrenner was responsible.

The first among baseball owners to understand the importance of the free-agent market, he plunged into it with daring and acumen. There were inevitable mistakes (Don Gullett, Rawley Eastwick), but

< 20 >

acquisitions like Catfish Hunter, Reggie Jackson, and Tommy John brought the Yankees pennants and profits. Then for reasons *still* known only to Steinbrenner, he decided after the Yankees lost the 1981 World Series not merely to shuffle players but to abandon the team's classic *modus operandi.* The Yankees, a power team since the days of "Murderers' Row," would opt for speed.

On the face of it, this was a risky move. The American League is still very much a natural-grass league and doesn't reward speed the way the Astroturf-heavy National League does, and Yankee Stadium is a left-handed power hitter's park. But Steinbrenner is no respecter of history, and he went at his chosen mission with characteristic vigor: Good-bye, Reggie Jackson; Hello, Dave Collins. In a single season, the Yankees plunged from the World Series to .488, escaping the ignominy of last place by only a single game.

Steinbrenner is not a stupid man (it is necessary to point this out only because he has done—quite visibly—so many stupid things), and before the 1982 season was a month old, he realized he'd made a serious strategic error. But by then, it was too late. Acquiring John Mayberry was a nice gesture, a sort of public *mea culpa,* but he was no longer the batting threat he'd been five years earlier, and it was inevitable that Steinbrenner would spend the time between seasons dipping mightily into the free-agent well.

But the rules of that game had changed considerably since the days of his spectacular successes. Other owners had learned how to play the free-agent market, and the multiplying breed of player agents had learned a few tricks as well; it was no longer like sitting down at the poker table with a bunch of Carmelite nuns. Multiyear contracts—five or six years in duration except for the oldest players—were now the norm; and once the settlement of the 1981 strike had demonstrated that free agency was going to be around for the foreseeable future, there were more owners actively bidding for blue-chip talents when they came up.

That strike occurred because the most conservative owners were trying to undo the free-agency rights that the players had previously won, and the blasting of their hopes for player-for-player compensation had a second key effect—at least in the mind of a shrewd game-player like Steinbrenner. It meant that any club facing the loss of a free agent, either because it didn't want him or because it didn't want

< 21 >

to pay him what other clubs might, was going to do its damnedest to trade that player to a club that *could* sign him. In other words, the example set by Minnesota, Cincinnati, and Charlie Finley's Oakland was likely no longer to be an aberration but the almost certain norm. In turn, that meant any ball club aggressively attempting to restructure itself had better sign quality free agents (or trade for potential free agents) whenever they came up—*whether or not the need for them was immediate.* Thus, the case of Don Baylor.

Though the argument could be made (and indeed *was* made quite vigorously at the time Baylor was acquired) that the Yankees needed another dh just about as badly as Buffalo needs more snow, the case is not entirely convincing. Yes, the Piniella/Gamble/Murcer combine was at least as effective as Baylor had been, but the Yankee triumvirate had problems of its own. Murcer was going to be thirty-seven years old in 1983, and in 1982 had only 141 at bats. He hit a respectable 7 home runs, but they represented almost a quarter of his 32 hits. His age and his .227 batting average made it look as though he wouldn't be back. Piniella, even older, was already forty, and though he batted a healthy .307 last season (including an even healthier .361 with men in scoring position), toward the end of the season his productivity tailed off dramatically; he had only 6 fewer hits in the second half of the season, but his r.b.i.'s fell from 25 to 12. A prudent owner could be excused for thinking—could indeed be blamed for *not* thinking—that Piniella's career was nearing its end.

But what about Oscar Gamble? With 18 home runs, 57 r.b.i.'s, and a .272 batting average (higher than his career .270), there's no evidence that he'd started to fade. There's not even any evidence that the Yankees would have been disadvantaged if they'd had to play Gamble against left-handers. Though he had only 34 at bats against lefties during 1982, he hit three homers, drove in ten runs, and batted .353. And at thirty-four, Gamble was actually six months younger than Baylor. Why wouldn't the Yankees want him to be their full-time dh?

They would. But so would any number of other teams, and Gamble would be eligible to enter the free-agent market at the end of the 1983 season—at which time he would probably be the premier dh available. If the Yankees didn't have a Baylor (or if one didn't develop unexpectedly from the farm system), they'd have to go all-out to get Gamble,

< 22 >

spending *at least* as much money for him as they had for Baylor, and there'd be no guarantee they'd succeed.

There are, of course, ball clubs that have waited, successfully, for their farm systems to produce the talent they need, but the Yankees aren't among them. Steinbrenner's decisiveness, combined with the previous Met management's ineptitude, had enabled him to snatch the New York market away from his National League rival, but the costs had been high. Not only did the Yankees have one of baseball's highest payrolls, they were loaded with long-term contracts and deferred payments to players that stretched decades into the future. To meet these contractual obligations, the Yankees needed a revenue stream based on at least two million fans a year; in other words, to pay for Steinbrenner's *past* winners, they needed at least to be present contenders.

Inevitably, then, the Yankees could never be the sort of team that develops organically but would be more like a cast assembled to perform in a particular movie. The problem, however, is that long-term contracts meant that the key performers—the leading men, if you will—would neither be available nor automatically disband at the same time. Steinbrenner, perhaps even more than other owners who'd gone the free-agency route, had to grab what he could, when he could. If that meant the 1983 Yankees—looking ahead a season—had a half-dozen romantic leads and no ingenues or character actors, so be it. If things don't work, a producer can always fire the director.

< 23 >

3

Video Games

Just before the Yankees left Florida, Steinbrenner met briefly with the team, wished them luck, and told them that if things went well he wouldn't see them until the All-Star break. It took him less than twenty games to decide that things weren't going well, and he joined them in Texas at the end of April. In that series' opening game, Martin had drawn an early ejection, and had signaled his displeasure with the thumb by kicking dirt at plate umpire Drew Coble. Though Steinbrenner said when he arrived at Arlington that he was "concerned for Billy," that was as close as he came to criticizing Martin's juvenile performance.

He was much more directly critical of his team. The Yankees had gotten off to an extremely slow (2–5) start, and had barely struggled to .500 by the time they reached Texas. After watching them lose their second straight game there, Steinbrenner announced that if he was going to lose he "could do it with kids from Columbus." With the team at 9–11, a record precisely what it had been a season earlier, he met first with Martin, then with the team. The most visible result of the first meeting was that Cerone, whose name Martin had already put on the lineup card, was scratched in favor of Wynegar. Steinbrenner had come to Texas armed with statistics showing that Wynegar, with

< 24 >

a batting average of .600, was the team's leading hitter with men in scoring position and that Cerone, then mired in an 0-for-15 slump, had been 0-for-6 with men in scoring position. The chief result of the second meeting and of Martin's comments to the players following it, as we shall later see, was the manager's notorious confrontation with Henry Hecht.

What apparently *didn't* happen during either of these meetings, despite Steinbrenner's announced "concern," was a request from the owner that his manager ease up on the umps a little bit. If anything, the evidence rather persuasively suggests that Steinbrenner enjoyed Martin's performances. He was, of course, still smarting from the record $50,000 fine Bowie Kuhn had slapped on him for his remarks in Florida about the National League umpires, but he had been convinced, long before that incident and its aftermath, that umpire-baiting was good business. Among his announced reasons for rehiring Martin had been that "Billy puts fannies in the seats," and the cover of the Yankees' media guide featured a caricature of Martin jumping up and down and angrily waving his finger in an umpire's face. And indeed, the videotapes from Martin's Texas performance promptly became part of a Yankees' television commercial.

This was not the only use the Yankees' owner had been making of videotapes. He had instructed Bill Bergisch, the team's vice-president for baseball operations, to send the league office copies of every disputable umpires' decision that went against the Yankees—together with critical comments. Other teams occasionally send such tapes, and virtually all teams from time to time are asked to provide them, but none do so with the metronomic regularity of the Yankees.

Occasionally, of course, televised replays do indeed show an umpire blowing a play, but in 98 cases out of 100 they demonstrate either that the original call was correct or that the play was so close the call at least *could* have been correct. The sensible operating rule followed by the reporters who see hundreds of such replays during the course of a season is that unless the tape unambiguously shows that the umpire was wrong, he was right. Given the pervasiveness of that feeling not only among reporters but among most baseball professionals, one might have thought that the deluge of Yankee-supplied tapes flowing into the league offices was merely harassment. That's certainly the way the umpires regarded it—with, it often appeared, some negative

< 25 >

consequences for the Yankees—but on May 27 it became apparent that the Yankees' owner thought of "the magic of video" as more than a metaphor.

The Oakland A's were at the Stadium that Friday night, opening a four-game series against the Yankees, and in the bottom of the first A's pitcher Mike Norris came high and very inside to Winfield. Winfield, who had already been tossed from one game for chasing Detroit's Dave Rozema after a similar pitch, quickly got up and turned toward the mound. In what was clearly a miscalculation (as well as a failure to follow established procedures), umpire Darryl Cousins stayed behind the plate instead of positioning himself between the dumped batter and the mound. With no one blocking Winfield, and with Winfield yelling threats at his pitcher, A's catcher Mike Heath stepped forward to intervene.

Though I watched the event live and over and over on tape, I regret to say I cannot tell precisely what happened. One player surely laid hands on the other, and one or the other escalated the touch into a shove, but the identity of the initial aggressor remains unclear, because during the critical moments the camera cut to the mound for Norris's reaction. What was unambiguously clear, however, was that at some point Winfield took Heath by the throat (virtually the only place he could grab him, given the catcher's mask and padding) and tossed him aside. At that point Cousins, who had by then inserted himself in the proper position, ejected Winfield.

But not Heath. The fans booed. Martin, who'd already been on Cousins for his ball-and-strike calls in the Oakland first, jumped out of the dugout to complain, but the single ejection stuck. Within a few moments, Winfield was in the locker room, and the game continued.

Steinbrenner, while all this was going on, was at home in Tampa, watching the game via satellite, and in a partly understandable rage —he does not like to see his most valuable player first endangered and then expelled—he called league president Lee MacPhail at home, complaining that Heath hadn't been ejected. This was imprudent, perhaps, and more than a trifle silly, but its imprudence was as nothing compared to what followed. As soon as he'd got off the phone with MacPhail, Steinbrenner called the Stadium press box and dictated a statement for press secretary Ken Nigro to issue to the reporters.

Nigro, who winced as he heard it, advised Steinbrenner to recon-

< 26 >

sider, but the owner was adamant. In a long and noticeably discon-
nected statement (the late-night sort that Washington reporters politely describe as "rambling and incoherent"), Steinbrenner not only
excoriated the umpires but also claimed that MacPhail had told him
he "could not understand why Mike Heath was allowed to stay in the
game."

This statement was circulated about the third inning, and by the
seventh Bob Fishel, MacPhail's assistant, had appeared in the press
box with the league's response. MacPhail began by dismissing Steinbrenner's version of their conversation: "It is absolutely untrue that
I said I could not understand why Umpire Cousins ejected only
Winfield. It is impossible to understand all that happens on the field
simply by watching TV. . . ." He went on to say that he made his
judgments on incidents like this only after receiving the umpires'
reports and reports from the league supervisors who were present.

He had no choice but to make such a response—as Steinbrenner
must certainly have known—because of the increasing militancy of
the umpire's union over the past decade under the leadership of Richie
Phillips. An allegation that the league president was issuing criticisms
of umpires solely on the basis of commercially televised reruns simply
could not be allowed to stand uncontested, or the league might very
well face an umpires' strike. Even if his version of what MacPhail had
said was accurate, Steinbrenner had painted MacPhail into a corner
by making it public, and MacPhail was furious. Since he believed
Steinbrenner's version had been willfully inaccurate, he was doubly
so, and his statement further said that "Mr. Steinbrenner's intemper-
ate blast is completely unacceptable and will result in disciplinary
action against him."

One might imagine that a message of this sort from the league
president would cause even the most imprudent owner to consider a
dignified retreat. One might further imagine that even Steinbrenner
would be somewhat placated by the fact that the Yankees went on to
win the game. One would be wrong, however, for Steinbrenner was
clearly off in some private zone of anger, and after the game was over
he came forth with a message of defiance. "This is still a free country,"
he said in part, "and we are free to express our opinions as far as I
know unless Lee MacPhail has authored a new Constitution and Bill
of Rights for the United States."

< 27 >

Two days later, MacPhail suspended Steinbrenner for a week. Though he vowed to "continue to speak out in defense of my players," Steinbrenner accepted the suspension meekly enough. He did this even though there was considerable legal doubt over whether the league president had the right to suspend an owner or whether that right was reserved to the commissioner. This was the first time in the history of baseball that such a suspension had been meted out, and Steinbrenner certainly had the option of appealing it to the commissioner. (One reason he might not have done so was that Kuhn had apparently been considering a *two-month* suspension for Steinbrenner's spring training remarks, but after determining that Steinbrenner wouldn't appeal had instead fined him $50,000—a sum ten times greater than the maximum technically allowed for such offences). Thus, with the season less than two months old, the Yankees had compiled an astonishing record that included two ejections, a $5,000 fine and a two-day suspension for the manager, and a $50,000 fine and a one-week suspension for the owner—all for complaints about the umpires.

Not surprisingly, some of the players were worried that the team might also have incurred the enmity of those umpires as well, and Martin, at least, deliberately cooled himself out, picking up only one more ejection over the course of the season. Indeed, he wound up finishing behind both the White Sox's Tony LaRussa and the Indians' Pat Corrales (who managed to get thrown out five times in less than half an American League season). Yet, because of Steinbrenner, who determined the Yankee organization's response to allegedly bad calls and unfair treatment, there was a crucial difference in the way Martin's outbursts were perceived. As MacPhail had written in his order suspending Steinbrenner, "the American League has experienced repeated problems with Mr. George Steinbrenner's mode and philosophy of operating the Yankees with respect to the umpiring of games. This philosophy has been apparent in their publications and their television commercials, in actions on the field, and in the public statements of Mr. Steinbrenner." After noting that the supervision of umpires was a league responsibility, MacPhail continued, "While I welcome constructive criticisms and suggestions from any of the clubs, I will not accept constant negativism from one club which includes public tirades. . . ."

< 28 >

In suspending Steinbrenner, MacPhail had put himself on the owner's enemies list, virtually guaranteeing that every ruling he subsequently made would be considered part of an anti-Yankee pattern. This would have important consequences in the wake of the pine-tar decision, when some of Steinbrenner's comments tipped so far over the borders of rationality that even Martin, hearing of one veiled threat, shook his head disbelievingly and asked, "Did he say *that?*" Yet the judgments in the suspension order were fair. Other owners might have tolerated umpire-baiting, but only Steinbrenner thrived on it. As Cousins himself said a couple of days after the Winfield-Heath incident, "This wouldn't be a big deal anywhere but New York."

It became a big deal because of Steinbrenner, of course, but his outburst was in some ways predictable; if it hadn't happened at this time, it would almost certainly have happened later. What is genuinely *weird* about this one, however—and what distinguishes it from, say, his spring training charges against National League umpires—is that this blast was precipitated by something Steinbrenner didn't see, and indeed could not have seen. At the moment the umpire was deciding who had been the aggressor when Winfield and Heath started shoving, the television cameras were focused elsewhere. The basis of his attack was therefore an unperceived event; one might strain and call what Steinbrenner "saw" merely wishful thinking, but it would more usually be described as a delusion. This was, even for Steinbrenner, a first.

< 29 >

4

Billy's Back

There is, then, no exaggerating the strangeness of life with Steinbrenner. Yet to a certain extent, as a look at the Yankees' roster problems makes clear, the changing rules under which the *business* of baseball is played has exacerbated, perhaps even institutionalized, the endemic conflict between a team's manager and its front office. It's not only on the Yankees that such conflicts escalate; this year, for instance, the Phillies fired their manager in midseason, even though the club was in first place at the time. But the Yankees are special, and not simply because of the incendiary chemistry between Martin and Steinbrenner. Though it requires a nearly superhuman effort of sociological vision to imagine the 1983 Yankees *without* that chemistry, the exercise is more than just an intellectual parlor trick. Aside from George, aside from Billy, the Yankees are *still* different from virtually every other major league club.

They are, for instance, one of only four pairs of teams competing within a common geographical area. No matter where it happens, the competition is real—depending on which team has been winning, the San Francisco Giants and Oakland A's have each been in trouble from time to time—but it is stronger in New York than elsewhere. Both Yankee Stadium and the Mets' home at Shea are accessible at the

< 30 >

same cost on the same subway system. And New Yorkers, unlike Bay Area residents, are accustomed to using mass transit. Moreover, though cable TV has recently made some inroads on the practice, there is almost always at least one baseball game available for free, on home television, every night of the season. While the attractions of the competing team may be minimal to any committed Met or Yankee fan, thousands of actual (and thousands more potential) ticket buyers lack such allegiance. When planning to take the kids to a ballgame, they will schedule whichever promises to be more interesting; when the choice is between heading out to the park or staying nome to watch a game on TV, they are likely to follow the team that's in a pennant race.

In general, even on a club that includes as many sideshows as the Yankees, "interest" is determined by the team's place in the standings. The manager could be among the earth's princes (Joe Torre or Bob Lemon, to take examples not at random), but if he doesn't win, he's gone. Though the Mets are often seen as a model of stability when compared to the circus Steinbrenner operates in the Bronx, it's well to remember that at the close of the 1983 season they named their fourth manager in the last five years.

True, Steinbrenner makes pikers even of the Mets (no one in base-ball has ever jettisoned managers with such theatrical flair), and equally true, no winning manager in the history of the game has ever been fired so often, by so many different owners, as Martin. But the reasons for this year's conflicts between Martin and Steinbrenner—minor only by the remarkable standards they've set in the past—aren't solely a function of their personalities. Much of what goes on between them has to do with how the organization works on a daily basis—and perhaps even more, as we shall see, with the exaggerated fishbowl-effect which is the Yankee environment.

One can't entirely separate the Yankees' organization chart from the owner's personality—he made it that way because he likes it that way—but it's marked by extreme thinness at the higher executive levels. Even when various title-bearing bodies have been in residence in the executive suites, Steinbrenner has been a hands-on owner. The California Angels have been at least as aggressive in the pursuit of free agents as Steinbrenner, but Gene Autry has left virtually all of the major baseball decisions to Buzzy Bavasi. And Bud Selig, of the

< 31 >

Milwaukee Brewers, while fully Steinbrenner's equal in energy and commitment, has let general manager Harry Dalton guide the club. But at least since the departure of Gabe Paul after the 1977 season, Steinbrenner himself has made *every* important Yankee decision (and most of the frivolous ones as well). When the Yankees were courting Reggie Jackson, for example, it was Steinbrenner himself who did the wining and dining; and this year, when the Yankees' computer revealed some disquieting batting stats for Rick Cerone, it was Steinbrenner who went to Texas and personally brought the figures to his manager's attention. Until Murray Cook was named as general manager shortly before the All-Star break this season (and there is little evidence so far that Cook's title is not going to be revealed as largely ceremonial), no significant buffer stood between the manager and the owner. When one was displeased by something, the other knew it without the mediation of any institutional shock absorber. Indeed— and here again the problem is not exclusively of personality—the communication of unhappiness was often achieved not through a third party whose interests lay with the smooth functioning of the team, but through a group of third parties who fed on conflict.

By and large, the reporters who regularly cover the Yankees both know and care a great deal about the game of baseball. They take genuine pleasure in watching a well-played game, and while the ancient command of "no cheering in the press box" is honored, there's a lot of *appreciating* going on; only Jane Gross of the *New York Times,* a specially talented interviewer, seems indifferent to the game's subtle beauties. With that exception, the beat reporters would rather write about baseball than about anything else; instead, they write about the Yankees.

The distinction is real, and while it too may be rooted in the interstices of the George-and-Billy Show, it has by now become institutionalized, and as a result the Yankees operate under the kind of media scrutiny more normally associated with summit conferences. Though the story he or she files on any given day may with luck cover only who played, who won, and how (and perhaps some suggestions why), each Yankee beat reporter routinely arrives at the Stadium three hours before game time. They do so not because they find any particular joy in hanging around the locker room as the players

< 32 >

wander in and dress, but because they are afraid they'll miss some critical aspect of the sideshow if they don't. Their editors, and their readers, expect no less.

The intensity of this attention has, I think, an effect on the players, but it exists apart from them—it is a response to ten years of Yankee history during which Steinbrenner, as MC, and Martin, as occasional guest star, have not only made the news but been it. The New York region's newspaper market is still competitive enough, and sports fans remain important enough to newspaper circulation, that the breaking story of the owner-manager relationship is going to be covered even when there's nothing breaking.

Even if it weren't part of the reporters' job, which it is, an inevitable concomitant of the time they spend around the locker room is that they begin to develop relationships of mutual trust with a handful of players and coaches. *Which* players and coaches is largely a function of the individual reporter's personality, but every beat writer has at least a couple of people to whom he or she can ask difficult questions and get—even if off the record—honest answers. If there were fewer papers covering the team, the Yankee clubhouse might be as veiled as Minnesota's or Seattle's, but as things stand, almost nothing that concerns the Yankees is likely to remain a secret for long; there are simply too many competent reporters living with the team.

Which brings us back to that early-season meeting Steinbrenner had with the players in Texas. During it, the owner singled out a handful of players—among them relief pitcher George Frazier—for direct criticism. As soon as Steinbrenner left the meeting, however, Martin began to take issue with him. Defending his players from what he regarded as unwarranted attacks—or, at any rate, from attacks that were *his* to make—Martin wound up telling the team to "ignore" what the owner said. Though there was some suspicion (without much evidence) that Steinbrenner and Martin had thought up this scenario to show the players that the manager was on their side, all hands agree that the content of the meeting was supposed to be secret.

It wasn't, of course, and stories filed by all the traveling writers contained references to what had gone on. The most directly circumstantial account, however, appeared in a column by Henry Hecht of the *New York Post,* who hadn't even been in Texas. Steinbrenner read the story, and immediately after the Yankees' May 14 home game—

< 33 >

Martin's first game back after his suspension—called the manager to complain. Martin's end of the conversation was perforce shared with the reporters who were gathered around his desk for the usual post-game interview, and contained the phrases "No, I hadn't read it. . . . Henry, huh? . . . I'll take care of it tomorrow, George."

There is a more than passing suspicion that this phone call was also set up for the edification of the press. Steinbrenner is surely familiar enough with the postgame routine to know that Martin's office would be full of reporters when he made the call; moreover, Martin's habitual practice when calls come through at that time is to get off the phone with a quick "I've got the press here now, I'll call you back." On the one or two occasions he's either wanted or needed to take calls during interview time, he's asked the reporters to leave for a few minutes and closed his door. Thus, this public and doubly unusual demonstration of owner/manager solidarity was almost certainly staged.

A month or so later, this charade and its aftermath would produce consequences neither party could have forseen, but the call's immediate result was predictable: Martin was going to chew out Hecht. The manager, it should be noted, needed little encouragement to undertake this task. Hecht, who had covered the Yankees for years before graduating to a broader baseball beat, was a veteran of many run-ins with Martin. Along with Murray Chass of the *Times,* Hecht was one of the two reporters present at Martin's famous, double-edged comment about Jackson and Steinbrenner: "One's a born liar, the other's convicted"—and his story was partly responsible for Martin's 1978 departure from the Yankees. Also, in the Reggie/Billy wars that characterized that year, Hecht had generally taken Jackson's side. At various times when he'd felt stung, Martin had accused Hecht of the reporter's cardinal sin: making stories up. While Martin had never been able to make such charges stick, it's unquestionably true that Hecht often worked the clubhouse *looking* for signs that players were unhappy with Martin—and finding them. The long-term animus between the two was real, and though one hesitates to hold *Post* reporters responsible for the colorful horrors visited on their copy by the paper's headline writers, the title given to Hecht's 1983 season-ender, "Hey, Boss! Ax Billy," was a fair representation of its content.

Still, no one could have quite anticipated how vigorously Martin

< 34 >

was going to fulfill his promise to "take care of it tomorrow, George." Because of a persistent drizzle, batting practice was canceled before the Yankees May 15 game with the White Sox, and the players were all hanging around their lockers. So when Martin, in undershirt and uniform pants, emerged from the trainer's room and began shouting, "Hey, everybody, we have a meeting right here," he had no trouble drawing a crowd. As the reporters present—including Hecht—prepared to leave, Martin said, "No, no. You guys don't have to leave. I don't want any of you to leave." He looked directly at Hecht and said, "particularly this little prick right here."

"We had a meeting down in Texas," he rasped. "It was supposed to be a private meeting, and I think it was. At least I haven't read anything true about it in the papers. But I did read, in a column by a guy who wasn't even there, about some things that were *supposed* to have happened. Now I didn't ever say don't talk to writers, but I'm saying right now: Don't talk to Henry Hecht.

"There he is," shouted Martin, pointing an accusing finger at Hecht, who stood—as calmly as possible under the circumstances— perhaps ten feet away, "and if there was ever a fuckin' bastard, there he is. He's the worst fuckin' scrounge ever to come around this clubhouse. He doesn't care if he hurts you or gets you fired, he just wants to *use* you. He got me fired twice, and now he's trying to make it a third time. And if you talk to him, don't talk to me, 'cause I don't want to have anything to do with anyone who talks to this little prick."

"You're paranoid," said Hecht.

"I'm not paranoid. I don't have to be paranoid to see that you're a little prick. You're not welcome in my office. You can come into the clubhouse—I wouldn't ever take away a man's right to earn a living —but you're not welcome in my office because I don't trust a fuckin' thing you say."

"You can imagine what I think of you."

"I read about it in the papers every day, you asshole. I don't need to imagine it. You're not welcome in my office," he repeated as he marched past Hecht and toward the sacrosanct retreat, finally muttering, "If that little bastard comes in here, I'll put him in the fuckin' whirlpool."

Curiously, the incident seemed over as soon as the office door closed

< 35 >

behind Martin. Though it had been genuinely frightening for a moment—Martin has a violent history, and for all that he might have begun his attack as a show, he'd been so caught up by his own performance that by the time he was finished his face was contorted with rage—the players shrugged it off as routine and quickly went back to whatever they'd been doing. One or two stopped for a word with Hecht, and Willie Randolph, in the classic jock gesture, gave him a passing pat on the ass, but that was about it. Hecht, who'd had the presence of mind to reach for his notebook as soon as Martin had begun, finished his rapid scribbling apparently undisturbed and eventually drifted back to the press lounge.

There, inevitably, he was put in the unfamiliar position of being interviewed, and most papers ran stories or columns on the incident. But the story was a one-day wonder; there were no complaints to the American League office, no protests from the Baseball Writers Association, and in a week it was forgotten.

Nonetheless, it revealed certain truths about how the Yankees operate—especially if one doesn't buy the theory that Martin and Steinbrenner had stage-managed their Texas differences. Though he's deeply involved in the team's daily operations, Steinbrenner's access to them is frequently a long-distance one. He has a number of other business interests that demand his attention: his Cleveland-based shipbuilding company, a racetrack and hotel in Florida, and extensive real estate holdings. In addition, through much of the '83 season, he spent time with his seriously ill father. Even when he's not physically present, however, Steinbrenner has always kept a watchful eye on his most highly visible enterprise. For years, he'd listened to most Yankee games on the radio, and he'd recently had a dish installed at his Tampa home so that he could capture signals from all the Yankees' televised games. Moreover, he had used one or another of his subordinates to monitor the goings-on inside the clubhouse.

Knowing this, and predisposed to worry about conspiracies, Martin is acutely sensitive about what he calls "clubhouse spies," and from time to time during the season indicated his belief that Jeff Torborg, a holdover coach, was playing that role for Steinbrenner. I know of no evidence for this particular accusation, but also have little doubt that when Steinbrenner feels the need for information he has the means to procure it. The point, though, as the leaks about the Texas

< 36 >

meeting testify, is that Steinbrenner doesn't need *spies*. Day in and day out, at home and on the road, the Yankees are observed by at least a half-dozen reporters, and the total is often considerably higher. Though these people have different degrees of skill and sophistication —and different sources as well—not much gets by them. Anything of genuine importance, as well as much that is merely colorful, is going to find its way into print—and to Steinbrenner.

That's not to say that every possible nuance of clubhouse life appears in the papers—there are unstated assumptions about certain comments or situations existing only "for background"—but especially in a town where the hard-fought newspaper war between the *Post* and the *News* is a fact of life, nothing legitimate is held back. The only time during the year when reporters actually got together to decide how a certain story should be covered was a series of lunchtime conversations about the news that Martin was going to be hospitalized during the All-Star break for tests and perhaps exploratory surgery to treat rectal bleeding. At least partly because batting wizard Charlie Lau's cancer had just become public knowledge, the immediate assumption was to think that Martin's problem was similar, and perhaps even fatal. But two of the writers possessed off-the-record information that neither Martin's prognosis nor even his diagnosis was necessarily serious; largely for the humane reason of preventing inevitably frightening banner headlines, they shared that information, and the story was (correctly, as it turned out) downplayed. But that single incident stands out precisely because it was the exception. Though it may take a couple of days, competition insures that Steinbrenner can usually find out whatever he wants to know by reading the papers.

Steinbrenner's absences make him in some ways dependent on the media, but they have another effect which is at least as important. As the Hecht/Texas incident makes clear, Steinbrenner's distance from the club shields him to a great degree. Though the owner certainly seemed to be calling the shots from his end of the telephone line, it was Martin, undertaking to confront Hecht in person, who had the altogether riskier role. And even when Martin's not engaged in a public dressing-down in the Hecht mode—the sort of moment at which suppressed enmities might bubble to the top of his volatile personality—Martin is more or less constantly on display. In addition

< 37 >

to the daily postgame press conference, reporters are in and out of his office whenever the open door gives them the signal he's available. And on the road, of course, he and at least some of the reporters can be found at the same bars. Though even many of these late-night conversations are guarded, they are at least superficially friendly and presuppose a degree of mutual trust.

Oddly, Martin doesn't seem to know how to *use* this degree of access. Even in the overheated world of the New York media, a skillful manipulator could turn the press, or at least a significant portion of it, into an ally, but subtle manipulations are not Martin's strong suit. Operating in nearly constant full view, and often under pressures that are not entirely of his own making, he's given to outbursts of saying exactly what he's thinking. When he called umpire Dale Ford a "stone liar" one afternoon in Chicago, history made his comment irresistibly newsworthy. Testimony from independent and trustworthy witnesses suggests that the accusation was accurate as well, but for a man who had already been suspended once during the season—and who had been warned by the league office that any further umpire-baiting would be punished—it was surely impolitic.

Steinbrenner is almost never unintentionally impolitic. He sees the press on his terms, and only when he wants to; when he decided he didn't want to be overheard during spring-training games, he simply declared the area where he liked to stand off limits to reporters. Nobody wanders unannounced into his office, and he often communicates through written statements that assure him of saying only what he wants to say. Sometimes what he says is dumb—as in the suggestion that Lee MacPhail agreed with his contention that an umpire had blown a call—but it is almost always calculated. Reporters may *hear* of Steinbrenner doing something stupid or impetuous, but they *see* Martin's gaffes. They can, and do, write about the latter whenever they occur, but rumors, even eyewitness accounts, have to be checked out before they see print, and pressures of time or space mean that such stories often wither for lack of attention.

Two other aspects of Steinbrenner's situation need to be considered. The first, and more obvious, is that his comparative reticence combines with his very real power to make what he does choose to say almost automatically newsworthy. Writers who get a call from him with some bit of news are therefore grateful and likely to print what

< 38 >

he tells them. And when they've done so often enough, he begins to provide them information "on background." In a virtual parody of the Kissinger heyday, knowledgeable sports-page readers have come to understand that phrases like "high Yankee source" or "an important figure within the Yankee organization" invariably introduce a Steinbrenner leak. Which leaks, it must be said, reporters welcome—especially when they are exclusive and amount to scoops.

The second aspect, less immediately obvious, is that the relative unfamiliarity most reporters have with Steinbrenner enhances his already considerable manipulative skills. After a certain amount of time spent regularly covering any figure from Ronald Reagan to Mick Jagger, skilled reporters will develop a bullshit detector. They may not be able to tell you precisely *how* they know it, but they know when that person is lying to them. But that facility can only be developed with practice, which is something Steinbrenner effectively denies them.

Finally, even the handful of writers who know Steinbrenner well enough to have a functioning detector can sometimes be fooled. Because his eccentricities have been so highly publicized, people sometimes forget how smooth Steinbrenner can be. A graduate of prestigious Williams College, he was a successful executive long before he came to own the Yankees, and no businessperson moves as far up the economic ladder as Steinbrenner has without having polished an ability to obfuscate or bend the truth when the occasion requires. During the Watergate investigation, you may remember, he even managed to fool federal investigators for a while.

Compared to Steinbrenner, Martin is crude, a bumbler. An intelligent but inattentive high school student whose higher education came through the game of baseball—the game as it was played back when grass was green and necks were red—Martin may know more baseball than the new breed of college-trained reporters who follow his team, but in other ways he's often well out of his depth. When he attempts to flatter a male writer, for instance, it is usually by suggesting that the writer must be getting laid a lot. This is frequently not a winning approach.

Even when he has managed to establish a close relationship with a given writer (or when that writer, in order to develop Martin as a source, has allowed himself to be used), Martin seems not to know

< 39 >

what to do with that resource. During the 1983 season, for instance, Martin grew close to Dick Gutwillig, of the Westchester-Rockland chain, and—though both writers maintained an honest independence —Gutwillig's columns were as sure a reflection of Martin's state of mind as the *Daily News*'s Bill Madden's were of Steinbrenner's. The difference is that Steinbrenner husbanded his shots, saving them for various crises (usually of his own manufacture), and Martin dissipated his on comparatively minor matters like his unhappiness with his largely inherited coaching staff.

Taken together, these factors added up in one way: unless Steinbrenner grievously miscalculated a particular tactic, any time a conflict between him and his manager surfaced in the media, Martin would lose it. In June, Steinbrenner made just such a miscalculation.

By the time the Yankees were finishing the homestand that opened the month, Steinbrenner had pretty well lost patience with Martin. The lineup was still shifting almost every day, and though Martin claimed to see some virtues in the juggling, Steinbrenner didn't. He did see, however, that the Yankees were at 27–26, barely above .500, and in sixth place. He could hardly blame this situation on the high-priced players he had signed (in fact, when he'd made an effort in that direction in Texas, no discernible change had resulted), so it must have been the manager's fault. Maybe Martin was too lenient. Perhaps he needed to be shown how to toughen up. In which case, Steinbrenner would oblige. He ordered what amounted to a punitive workout in Milwaukee, taking away what would have been a day of rest for his players.

Despite his pious protestations when league president Lee McPhail ordered that the pine-tar game be finished on what would otherwise have been an off-day for the Yankees, Steinbrenner has long been a believer in extra workouts, and there was nothing outstandingly unusual about this order. Except that Martin either (his version) misunderstood it or (Steinbrenner's) willfully disobeyed it, making the workout mandatory for only a handful of players, voluntary for all the rest. When the day came, Martin himself was among the absent "volunteers."

He did, however, have a phone conversation with Steinbrenner, during which—according to Steinbrenner—Martin misled him, giv-

< 40 >

ing him the impression that except for one or two excused players, all the Yankees—along with Martin—had attended the workout. When Steinbrenner found out what had really happened (in this case, at least, *before* the story had been printed, leading one to believe that Martin's fear of clubhouse spies may have been prudent as well as paranoid), he shifted gears from annoyance to fury.

Suddenly, the papers, led by the *Daily News,* were ablaze with anti-Martin stories, some of them focusing on practices that had been standard for weeks: He wasn't on the field watching batting practice (true; he was often in his office talking with reporters or going over scouting reports on the Yankees' opponent); he was known to sleep in his office during the afternoons (true again, but he also usually showed up for work at about 11 A.M., nine hours before Yankee night games were scheduled to begin—for a fifty-five-year-old man to take a short nap breaking up what would otherwise be a fourteen- or fifteen-hour workday seems not so awful). New charges, which might not have been printed under happier circumstances, surfaced as well, most notably the story that during much of the Milwaukee series Martin seemed more interested in an attractive woman he'd installed in a box seat next to the dugout than in what was happening on the field (this, too, was true—and not susceptible to explanation). Also, the Yankees lost two of three.

By the time the team reached Cleveland, Steinbrenner's home port, the owner had made up his mind to fire Martin, and the episode in which a frustrated Martin smashed the dugout toilet with a baseball bat merely added to Steinbrenner's certainty. The two met, along with Martin's lawyer, Eddie Sapir, at the Pewter Mug restaurant, and while the details of that meeting remain in dispute (Martin said at the time that the meeting had "satisfied" Steinbrenner, which Steinbrenner, on the record, disputed), Steinbrenner's determination to get rid of his manager apparently remained unaltered. Certainly that's what he told his favored reporters *off* the record, and his statements to them were couched so strongly that the *Daily News* gave over its back page to a cartoon of Yogi Berra, the Yankees' "next" manager.

One thing apparently did become clear to Steinbrenner during that Cleveland meeting: under the terms of Martin's contract, nothing he'd yet done allowed the owner to fire him "for cause." If Steinbrenner did swing the ax, he would immediately owe his exmanager about 2.3

< 41 >

million dollars in salary Martin would otherwise have earned over the eight-year life of the contract. Thus, when the team arrived in New York, Steinbrenner didn't dismiss the manager; instead, he took the one action most likely to provoke Martin into quitting: he fired his pitching coach and longtime friend, Art Fowler. Steinbrenner expressed no complaints with Fowler's coaching abilities, saying only that he "thought Billy talked too much only to Art . . . not taking advantage of his other coaches."

Trying to find the one thing that would both humiliate and infuriate Martin, Steinbrenner hit the mark pretty well. Though Fowler's work as a coach gets mixed reviews (Guidry almost worships him, but another starter says Fowler's coaching consists entirely of instructions to "throw strikes," sometimes expanded to "Godammit, throw strikes"), his role as Martin's confidant was critical. Because he was the *only* coach Martin had chosen himself (contrary to usual baseball practice), he was the only one Martin trusted fully—the only one he could be certain wasn't a "clubhouse spy." Later in the season, Martin revealed that when he left Steinbrenner's office shortly after four o'clock that afternoon, he was indeed thinking of quitting. Steinbrenner had played his cards well.

At that point, Martin, upset and frustrated, did a stunningly stupid thing. He had entered the clubhouse through a side door and had gone into his office, where he'd placed a call to Sapir. By this time, his head was starting to ache, and he was feeling depressed, so he left his office and went across the locker room to get some medicine from the trainer. On his way back, he saw an attractive young woman sitting at one of the clubhouse tables, chatting with his players. Assuming at first that she was someone's guest, he ordered her from the room. By the time he learned differently—that she was a *New York Times* researcher gathering information for that paper's annual compilation of the players' all-star team—he had already escalated beyond control. Loudly, obscenely, he chased her out.

Martin went back into his office, closing the door behind him (it would stay closed until after reporters had been routinely cleared from the clubhouse a half-hour before game time). The researcher, Deborah Henschel, decided to go over to the visitor's clubhouse and distribute questionnaires to the Brewers. On the way across the field, however, she was stopped by one of the Stadium's notoriously offi-

< 42 >

cious security guards, who challenged her credentials and barred her access. Prevented from doing her assignment—and believing, not illogically, that Martin had somehow had a hand in the guard's activity—she telephoned her desk for instructions. Wait upstairs at the executive offices, she was told, the *Times* would take care of things. The deputy sports editor called the Yankees.

Steinbrenner himself took the call, eventually bringing the researcher into his office and getting her version of the story in detail. While Martin was downstairs alone, still brooding over Fowler and not yet recognizing the significance of his later actions, Steinbrenner was being told that his manager—an official spokesman for the New York Yankees—had not only ejected an accredited member of the media from his clubhouse but had also suggested that she suck his cock. Steinbrenner apologized to her. He apologized to the *Times.* He did not, so far as anyone knows, dance a jig around his desk, but under the circumstances such glee wouldn't have been inappropriate. This was manna from heaven. If Martin had indeed done what the researcher had said he had, Steinbrenner wouldn't have to wait for him to quit. He could be fired. For cause.

We will have here a brief digression, a sort of rain delay, if you will, while we consider the question of what made this incident so spectacularly more important than the earlier blowup with Henry Hecht. Was it simply that George was already mad at Billy? That the *Times* is institutionally more powerful and palatable than the *Post?*

Neither of these factors can be discounted, but the real difference is more fundamental and altogether creepier. It has to do with baseball's continuing Weenie Question.

Martin, it was alleged, told the woman from the *Times* to "suck my dick," as he ejected her from the clubhouse. The charge, though by no means proven, was inherently plausible. Boys will be boys, after all, and locker rooms will be locker rooms. Martin himself admitted he told her to get her ass out of the clubhouse, and reliable witnesses to the incident said he added that if she was unhappy with his edict, she (or perhaps her employer, there was some conflict here) could "kiss my dago ass." Within that context of hostility, the distinction between ass-kissing and cocksucking seems academic, but in a jesuitical narrowing of the issues that was truly wondrous to behold, it was

< 43 >

precisely on that distinction that Martin's tenure as Yankee manager came to rest.

Consider, for instance, the comments of the fifty-two-year-old Perfect Shipbuilder to a crowd of male and female reporters later on in that turbulent weekend. "If a girl's going to come into the locker room, she's going to have to take 'get your ass out of here,' " he said, "but that other thing . . ." He paused coyly, "You girls hold your ears," then lowered his voice. "You know what it was. It involved the word 'suck.' . . . If someone had said that to *my* daughter, I would have shot the guy."

This is, I promise, all true (after Steinbrenner had left, a group of us checked our stunned disbelief by reading our notes back and forth to each other). Despite what anyone attempting to impose a degree of rationality on this circus might have thought, the problem was indeed the Weenie Question.

Male baseball players, you see, have (cover your ears, girls) weenies. Allowing for variations of right and left dress, these may be said to hang down between baseball players' legs and are visible (though except in rare cases unremarkable) when players are unclothed. Since the Lords of Baseball long presumed that ladies would faint at the sight of a weenie—and that females of lower degree would be grabbing at them all the time—women reporters were for years barred from major league clubhouses. Sports desks, notoriously the most conservative of newspaper bureaus, gladly collaborated in the discrimination that made the job of women reporters doubly difficult, but eventually a few papers and magazines lurched into the seventies. Having hired women as reporters, they began to complain when their writers weren't allowed to function, and still more eventually (after lawsuits and despite harassment whose grotesque details are neatly reported in Roger Angell's *Late Innings*), women reporters were allowed the same access as their male colleagues.

More often than not, however, their equality remains only superficial. It took years for baseball to adjust to the post–Jackie Robinson era (and Calvin Griffith *still* doesn't have it quite right), and in that instance, players and executives were dealing with men whom they were forced to admit were their athletic equals. Since many players —particularly on teams like the Yankees, which in times of crisis are besieged by reporters whose ignorance of baseball is, or at least ought

< 44 >

to be, embarrassing—routinely hold *all* reporters in a generalized contempt, it's going to be at least as long a time before women writers stop being victimized by false chivalry and the madonna-whore paradigm.

Martin, it seems safe to say, is not going to be a leader in the march toward the future. In a classic blaming-the-victim speech, he smirkingly described the researcher as "sprawled out there across the table like a hussy, with a dress split all the way up to her hind end. . . . It looked like she was a professional, put it that way." Since Martin is an equal-opportunity bully, his original attack, even if the most lurid versions of it were correct, was considerably less misogynistic than the repellent attitude revealed in his subsequent efforts at self-justification.

Such attitudes—perhaps in any male-dominated professional sport, and certainly in baseball under the aegis of George Steinbrenner—are inevitably going to make their ugliness felt, for the Steinbrenner ethic effectively *encourages* uncontrolled emotional outburst. Martin's taking a baseball bat to a toilet may have been a first, but how many times have you read apparently approving stories of disappointed batters smashing a water cooler. Somehow, in the Yankees' insulated world, the temper tantrum doesn't prove that you're bonkers but only that you *care*. In the real world, grownups—legislators whose pet bills go down, corporate executives outmaneuvered by a rival firm—don't get rewarded for breaking the furniture. But Steinbrenner had given at least tacit approval to Martin's vulgar attack on Hecht, and had himself once attempted to fire up his troops by fighting a famous boxing match with an elevator. That a world which considers incidents like these normal would still be vexed by the Weenie Question seems perfectly fitting.

As soon as Steinbrenner got the phone call from the *Times,* he had Martin where he wanted him. He could probably have fired him on the spot—or at least immediately after the game—and gotten away with it. But there might then have been the possibility of litigation, and Steinbrenner wanted to be protected. What he needed was someone else to find Martin guilty; then he could move unchecked. During an interview the next day with Bill Madden of the *News,* Steinbrenner found his opportunity, and asked if the Baseball Writers Association of America was going to request an investigation. Mad-

< 45 >

den said he didn't know but thought one might be appropriate, as the BBWAA had a long-standing concern that accredited members of the media not have their access to stories limited by the whims of a manager. When the interview concluded, he went off to telephone the New York chapter chairman, Moss Klein of the *Newark Star-Ledger.*

Unable to reach Klein (who in any case would have refused to request such an investigation on the grounds that no protest had been lodged when Hecht—unlike Henschel, actually an association member—had been barred from the manager's office), Madden called a *Daily News* colleague, Jack Lang, the national secretary-treasurer of the BBWAA. Madden and the *News,* it should be remembered, were further out on the "Billy fired" limb than any other area newspaper, and an investigation that wound up discrediting Martin would make the paper's stories announcing his demise retroactively correct. Whatever prompted Lang, he got in touch with BBWAA president Randy Galloway of the *Dallas Morning News,* and Galloway sent a letter to American League president Lee MacPhail asking that the league investigate the incident and that "proper disciplinary action follow." Galloway read a copy of the letter over the telephone to Bob Fishel in MacPhail's office, and the league agreed to the BBWAA request.

On Saturday night, Steinbrenner was still apparently in the catbird seat. He'd met with Martin and heard the manager's side of the story, and Martin, at least, felt that Steinbrenner believed him; he told reporters that things were "okay." Steinbrenner, through his press secretary, issued a statement saying that "by no means is everything okay," adding that "we will continue to cooperate with the league in its investigation."

Though Steinbrenner obviously believed the investigation would serve his interests in the long run—otherwise, he wouldn't have subtly arranged for it—in the short run, it froze his hand. He could hardly claim to be cooperating with an investigation and fire Martin before the results were in. But a couple of unpredictable things happened while the investigation was still going on. First, the Yankees swept the Milwaukee series, and second, during the game after the news of the Martin/*Times* incident had broken, the fans twice delayed play with applause for Martin—initially when he trotted out with the trainer to check on Steve Kemp after the outfielder had run into the wall, and later, and even more remarkably, when a picture of Martin appeared

< 46 >

on the Stadium's Diamondvision scoreboard.

These were perhaps unsettling, but manageable. What was *not* manageable was something Steinbrenner fatally miscalculated: the behavior of the *Times*. For a number of sound First Amendment reasons, the *Times* doesn't allow its news employees to participate in investigations carried on by outside agencies. What the paper prints is on the record; everything leading up to the printed story is privileged. *Times* reporters have gone to jail defending this principle, and it was not going to be compromised simply because a *Times* employee had in her professional capacity played a role in the incident being investigated. The American League asked for permission to talk with Henschel, even on an informal basis, but their request was firmly denied.

The decision by the *Times* did not serve Henschel well; it left her twisting in the wind, with no way to get her side of the story on record, but no one (with the possible exception of Steinbrenner) would argue that the paper was wrong to stay aloof from the investigation. Whether cooperation with this investigation would actually jeopardize the newspaper's ability to protect itself, its reporters, and their sources from less warranted and more threatening intrusions is a matter for lawyers to decide. The *Times* lawyers thought it could, and that was enough.

Steinbrenner had outsmarted himself. With the star witness silent and a number of locker-room witnesses saying that they, at least, hadn't heard Martin urge the fellation that dare not speak its name, the results of the investigation became a foregone conclusion. On Tuesday, barely four days after the incident, the league president issued his report: "Based on the information we have been able to gather, I must hold that there is no cause for serious disciplinary action against Mr. Martin. The American League does not approve of language he used, but the language used does not far transcend language used in a professional baseball clubhouse."

This was a Scottish verdict, certainly, but because Martin's job had come to hang upon the precise form of insult he'd used, "not proven" was good enough to save him—for a while.

< 47 >

5

Brain (Mis)Trust

If the Yankee bench was so overflowing with quality players that it was sometimes embarrassing, the depth of their coaching staff had progressed beyond embarrassment and into the realm of ludicrousness. Through most of their history, the team had been heavily staffed —going first-class in every way was part of the Yankee aura—but under Steinbrenner, the ancillary staff began to push against the limits of plausibility. In addition to a generous handful of part-timers who show up when the team is at home, the Yankees travel with a batting-practice catcher (which most teams regard as a needless luxury) and two batting-practice pitchers—one left-handed, one right-handed (on most teams, coaches throw bp). To be sure, these three have other duties—operating the videotape, computer, and radar gun, as well as charting the pitches—but they, along with the Yankees' special bullpen catcher (a position ordinarily filled by the second or third catcher on the roster), pick up a great deal of what would normally be coaches' work. This might theoretically appear to free the coaches for more important work, but at least as Martin had organized things at the beginning of the season, there wasn't that much to be done. Not that hitting fungoes to fielders isn't important enough in its way, but only a couple of people can do it at any one time. Besides, its not

< 48 >

exactly what you could call *demanding* work. To a great extent, many of the coaches seemed to be fifth—or maybe sixth—wheels.

Some of this had to do with the nature of the Yankees. On clubs that play a lot of rookies, or that at least carry several on their roster, coaches are needed as teachers as well as baseline traffic cops. But the Yankees were so loaded with veteran players that instruction ranked relatively low on the club's priority list. Primarily, however, the coaching staff seemed otiose because Martin made them so.

It's a baseball truism, and in general a sound administrative practice, that a manager picks his own coaching staff. A midseason replacement may keep an existing staff on for reasons of continuity; but if he survives into a second season, he chooses the men he'll be working with. This makes sense both philosophically—if the manager and the coaches think about baseball in contradictory ways, the team is going to be in trouble—and socially—for seven months of the year, these guys virtually live together, and if they're at each other's throats, the negative feelings will spill over into the team. Finally, the pressures of the job are such that the manager, any manager, needs a staff he can trust as a balance, or perhaps a support, to the dozens of difficult judgments each day brings. And a Yankee manager needs such people especially. With Steinbrenner second-guessing his every move, the Yankee manager not only needs a trustworthy sounding board for his ideas, he needs to be sure that his coaches' primary loyalty is to him—that they won't be feeding the owner's temptation to pick up the telephone and act as his own manager.

Martin had no such assurance. By the time he joined the Yankees in January of 1983, the coaching staff was virtually in place. Yogi Berra, one of the most popular players in Yankee history, was its senior member; he'd been back with the Yankees since 1976, and would be there as long as he wanted to be. Jeff Torborg, whom Steinbrenner had come to know and respect as manager of the Indians, had been bullpen coach since 1979 and had recently been given a five-year contract. Don Zimmer, with nine years of major league experience as a manager (and a solid 506–410 record in the American League) had been hired at the close of the '82 season to replace Joe Altobelli at third base. Finally, less than a week before rehiring Martin, Steinbrenner brought Roy White on board. White, a Yankee outfielder for more than a decade, had been playing in Japan for the

< 49 >

three previous seasons and had been offered a coaching slot in Cleveland by Mike Ferraro, himself a former Yankee third-base coach. White held him off, however, claiming that he was thinking of returning to Japan, while he was actually attempting to negotiate a three-year contract with Steinbrenner.

Though the appointment of White rankled somewhat, Martin—by then deep in conversation with Steinbrenner—didn't try to block the owner's decision. Instead, he concentrated on getting his own man, Art Fowler, as pitching coach. Initially, Steinbrenner resisted, for he regarded Martin's longtime bar partner as a negative influence. Like a lot of other people in baseball, Steinbrenner didn't have much regard for Fowler's credentials as a pitching coach, but in the intensive talks that preceded Martin's hiring Steinbrenner finally relented. Martin could have one coach of his own. If he wanted Fowler, that was all right.

At sixty, Fowler was five years older than Martin, but his active playing career had lasted nearly a decade longer. In 1963, two years after Martin had retired, the forty-one-year-old Fowler made 57 relief appearances for the California Angels, and when he was forty-eight he made 45 appearances and compiled a 1.59 e.r.a. as player-coach for the Minnesota Twins' Denver club. It was there that he met Martin, who was then beginning his managerial career, and their association had continued ever since. He coached for Martin at Minnesota in '69, at Detroit from '71 to '73, then at Texas, with the Yankees, and during Martin's three-season stint at Oakland. Even if Martin had been given a free hand to pick his own coaches, he couldn't have picked anyone in baseball who was closer to him than Fowler, for no such person existed.

Despite the negative rap that accompanied him, Fowler wasn't just Billy's buddy but a legitimate major league pitching coach. His strength lay less in mechanics, however, than in attitude. (Like many pitchers who'd been around baseball in the 1940s, Fowler *was* capable of teaching a spitter, and is widely given credit—or blame—for teaching Mike Torrez the wet one, but that's not the sort of thing a coach can put on his résumé. In a sense, however, it won the 1978 pennant for the Yankees when Torrez—then with Boston—hung one to Bucky Dent in the playoff.) As a result, Fowler's greatest successes have come not with struggling older pitchers but with youngsters who need

< 50 >

a jolt of self-confidence and savvy to get them going. At least over the short term, his work with the Oakland staff provided plenty of evidence that he's hardly the Bozo Steinbrenner thought he was, and Ron Guidry unabashedly describes Fowler as "the greatest pitching coach I've ever had." Not so incidentally, Guidry's only 20-game seasons ('78 and '83) came when he was coached for at least part of the year by Fowler. Dave Righetti, whose short Yankee career has given him experience with an unusually large number of coaches, is also a big Fowler booster.

But Guidry in '78, like Righetti in '83 (and like virtually the entire '80 Oakland staff), already had command of his pitches. What a young pitcher of that sort needs is the ability, and the courage, to throw his pitch, at his time, where he wants to. And this, Fowler could give.

Precisely how he managed it is something of a mystery. Fowler is by no means the most articulate of men, and even if he were, his syrupy Carolina drawl can be virtually impenetrable. Perennially flushed, with a prominent nose that has apparently spent a long time near the bottom of a whisky glass, Fowler certainly doesn't seem like the sort of father figure a tentative young rookie might choose. And when he did attempt actual instruction, his methods were, well, primitive.

Early in the season, when virtually all the Yankee pitchers were plagued by control problems that forced them to pitch with counts of 2–0 or 3–1, Fowler gathered his charges around him in the bullpen and issued a now famous edict: "Throw strikes." "It's easy," he continued, and setting up on the mound, threw twenty knee-high fastballs in a row to the bullpen catcher, alternating from the inside to the outside corner of the plate. "See?" he said, and the day's lesson was over.

Later on, in the clubhouse, Rudy May remarked that he too could throw a fifty-five-mile-an-hour fastball over the plate, but that there were about 150 hitters in the league he wouldn't particularly care to throw it to, at least "not without a helmet on, or maybe a suit of armor."

May is actually a classic example of a pitcher Fowler *couldn't* help (Martin, in fact, would argue that May was beyond help this year, but that's another matter). Through most of spring training, May was disastrously and almost incomprehensibly wild. Though he had, like

< 51 >

most curveball pitchers, a history that included occasional streaks of wildness, he'd shown remarkable control during the previous season, walking only 14 batters while striking out 85 over 106 innings. During the spring, however, he walked 12 in only eight innings—during which he also threw a couple of wild pitches. The sudden and mysterious loss of control failed absolutely to respond to Fowler's injunctions to throw strikes, and when they didn't work, Fowler had nothing left to fall back on.

Eventually, May began working with Sammy Ellis, a minor league pitching coach who was in camp as an instructor, and the two began to break down May's mechanics. When an experienced pitcher, coming off a good season, suddenly goes bad, it's a sign either of arm trouble—which may be beyond any coach's ability to cure—or of an unrealized change in the pitcher's motion. Working with films from preceding years, Ellis finally isolated a difference that might possibly be at the root of May's problem. In what was perhaps an unconscious attempt to hide the ball from the batter a little longer, May wasn't pulling his pitching hand out of his glove as early as he'd done when he was pitching successfully. The two practiced the new/old motion on the sidelines for a day or two, and Martin scheduled May to pitch an inning in the final preseason game against Kansas City. As it happened, the luckless left-hander's turn came round when the KC batting order was loaded with right-handers, but after missing with a 3–2 pitch to leadoff man George Brett, May closed out the inning with a pop-up and two strikeouts. After the game, even Martin, jealous of Fowler's role and skeptical about Ellis, admitted that May's performance was "real good to see."

But the problems with Fowler really had less to do with his coaching abilities—and here, one *does* have to remember Guidry and Righetti—than with his special relationship to Martin. Though Martin certainly used all his coaches heavily during the spring—he designed the plays, but the coaches drilled them, often when he was absent in his office or on another part of the field—he confided only in Fowler. Given the circumstances of his past hirings and firings, the narrowness of his trust was understandable, but it meant that key roster decisions in which he could have used some feedback and perhaps some additional counterarguments were made largely on his own. Further, by keeping the coaches at a distance from those decisions,

< 52 >

Martin unwittingly made himself more susceptible to Steinbrenner's second-guessing. If they'd been part of the process, the other coaches could at least have cited Martin's reasons when Steinbrenner asked them why certain players had been cut, as he did most particularly about Butch Hobson. But because they'd been essentially cut off, all they could honestly tell Steinbrenner was that while they could certainly see arguments for releasing Hobson, they really had no idea why Martin did what he did. They weren't told, and they didn't ask.

Not surprisingly, the lack of information frustrated Steinbrenner mightily, and rather than blaming Martin (whom he had, after all, hired) or himself (for putting Martin in a position where he could trust only one of his coaches), Steinbrenner blamed Fowler. He hadn't wanted to hire Fowler in the first place, and nothing that happened during the spring had changed his mind. As soon as he had even the hint of an excuse, Fowler was going to go.

As it happened, when he finally fired Fowler on June 17 ("asked him to assume other duties within the organization" was the official phrasing), Steinbrenner was trying to force Martin to quit, and so acted without even the semblance of an excuse. Guidry (9–4) and Righetti (7–2) were both off to excellent starts, and Shane Rawley, at 7–5, had an e.r.a. of 3.88, lower than it had been in either of the preceding two seasons. The rest of the starting rotation was a mess, to be sure, but that had pretty much been predictable; besides, the recent arrival of Matt Keough, with whom Fowler had had outstanding success at Oakland, might go a long way to changing that. Steinbrenner, however, simply snatched Fowler up by the feet and used him as a hammer to thwack Martin.

Roy White had actually been the first victim of the Martin-Steinbrenner conflict. For all his occasional disagreements with them, Martin was extremely careful not to criticize his coaches in public. Even after Don Zimmer's disastrous day at third in the crucial September series against Baltimore—in the 5–3 loss that effectively eliminated the Yankees from the pennant race, Zimmer twice sent home runners who were thrown out by several feet—Martin held his tongue, and Zim ("I had a horseshit day") was far harder on himself than the manager was.

Not so with White. Early in spring training, when White was in the coaching box at first, the rookie coach missed a sign. Though the

< 53 >

mistake was obvious enough, the culprit wasn't—not, at any rate, until Martin announced that White had screwed up, not for the first time, and that he was forthwith going to be replaced by Yogi Berra. All of a sudden, White had no discernible job. He hit his share of fungoes to the infielders and flies to the outfielders, even pitched an occasional turn at batting practice, but this proud man—one of the few class players on the Yankees during the Horace Clarke era—was doing nothing that couldn't be done equally well by Dom Scala, the bullpen catcher. White was a nonperson not for a week or two but for the entire season. Even when Berra came down with pneumonia and missed several games, he didn't get another shot at first base. Fowler, because he'd effectively been fired, was able to go home to Carolina and spare himself the embarrassment of the spurious "reassignment." But if White had quit in the face of his daily humiliation, he would have forfeited his salary, so he stuck it out. The closest he came to visible protest was his pointed refusal to ride in the same bus with Martin on any trip when there was a choice. Day in, day out, he was there—studying his racing form, placing a few bets, organizing locker-room pools for televised races, having an occasional evening beer with Piniella and Murcer, friends from his playing days. True, he had been dishonest with Mike Ferraro when Ferraro had offered him the Cleveland job, but he surely didn't deserve the treatment Martin gave him. No one could.

The strangest thing about all this was that Martin actually *liked* White. Martin had gone out of his way to say nice things about White as a player in his autobiography, *Number 1,* and he was particularly fond of White's son, Reade, who had been an occasional visitor in the manager's office when White was playing for Martin's Yankees. But once Fowler had been fired, any hope of a rapprochement vanished.

Obviously, Fowler's forced exit didn't do much for relations between Martin and the other surviving coaches either. Zimmer had gradually been earning Martin's respect and trust, but that process came to a quick halt, and the already fragile détente between Martin and Torborg was terminally fractured when Martin read a newspaper story saying that Steinbrenner had asked Torborg if he'd take the job when Martin was fired—and that Torborg had agreed. Martin, who knew Torborg was close to Steinbrenner, believed that story—and

< 54 >

believed as well that it was Torborg's criticisms of Fowler that had led Steinbrenner to fire him.

Torborg seemed, in every way except in popularity with the fans, a more likely candidate for the manager's job than Berra. A college graduate, with a master's degree he'd earned with a thesis on the effects of platooning in baseball, Torborg was polished, articulate, and, at forty-one, still boyishly handsome. He would obviously have been a "new breed" manager in the mode of Steve Boros or Rene Lachemann, but despite his gentlemanly surface, he was still very much a jock. A backup catcher for all but one of his ten major league years, Torborg retained something of a catcher's sense of humor. Not only did he more than hold his own in the clubhouse needling, he was fully capable of spiking George Frazier's uniform underwear with linament and roaring with laughter at the pitcher's athletic leaps of agony. Far closer to the players than Martin was, he was nonetheless careful to hide the dislike—a feeling that often seemed to border on contempt—he felt for the manager. Publicly, he could not have been more loyal to Martin, even giving him credit—where none was particularly due—for a share in the late-season resurrection of Bob Shirley.

He would not, however, submit to being yelled at. "I'm not sure why," he once mused, "there's probably a psychological explanation that's too upsetting for me to deal with, but I really *physically* can't stand it when someone yells at me. Even my wife knows not to do it."

Martin, whose emotions are constantly bubbling a bare millimeter below his skin, is a notorious screamer, and in an August game against the Tigers in Detroit he completely blew his stack when Dale Murray, despite instructions, threw a forkball to Alan Trammell. There were two out in the bottom of the ninth at the time; the Yankees had just rallied to take a one-run lead. But Murray not only threw the forkball, he hung it, and Trammell hit a game-tying home run. Martin, crazed with rage, grabbed the phone to the bullpen and started screaming into it: "What the fuck was he doing throwing the forkball? I told him not to throw the goddamn forkball. Don't you fuckin' tell those guys *anything* out there?" Martin was so fired up he initially failed to realize that it was Gossage and not Torborg who'd picked up the phone, but when that mistake had been cleared up and Gossage, holding the phone a safe distance from his ear, had called Torborg

< 55 >

over, Martin started right up again. Torborg listened for perhaps five seconds and then, in full view of the players who'd been watching the exchange with considerable interest, dropped the phone to the dirt and walked away.

Sammy Ellis, in the dugout with Martin, didn't have Torborg's option, but in a certain sense he had felt it was a victory when Martin finally began to yell at him. For the first few games after Ellis joined the Yankees as Steinbrenner's chosen replacement for Fowler, Martin simply ignored him. "I'm my own pitching coach," he said, tacitly threatening to turn Ellis into a Roy White. In the early stages of Ellis's return, Martin told his pitchers not to listen to him, and even refused to let Ellis go to the mound to settle down a troubled pitcher during games. But Ellis—partly because of his personality, partly because he had a genuine job to do and could do at least a part of it without Martin's cooperation—refused to knuckle under.

Instead, working with starting pitchers in their pregame warmups, talking strategy and tactics with them during their daily rounds of running, he gradually won their confidence. And when he and Torborg together made an adjustment in Dale Murray's motion that at least temporarily returned the right-hander's sinkerball to its past effectiveness, Ellis began to win Martin's as well. He appeared to gain it completely when, late in the season, he got a call from Murray Cook demanding some statistics about the number of pitches Guidry had thrown over his last several starts. Guidry had pitched a large number of complete games—some of them when he was obviously tiring and the result seemed settled—and there had been some newspaper criticism of Martin as a result. Ellis complied with the request (if he hadn't, Cook could simply have pushed a button on the Yankees' computer and had the figures delivered to him), but he also told Martin what Cook had been asking. From then on, completing a process which had begun to develop shortly after the All-Star break, Martin relied more and more on Ellis's judgments.

That did not, of course, wipe away Martin's memories, and when he read in a *Daily News* article that appeared after the Yankees had been eliminated that neither Torborg nor Ellis wanted to come back if he did, Martin fired from the hip. Neglecting to check whether the piece was accurate, he instead launched an attack on the two, telling some of the Yankee pitchers that the coaches *had* to come back:

< 56 >

"Where else are they gonna get a job? They couldn't even get hired in fuckin' *Egypt.*" Torborg, who'd been offended by the original article (whose source had apparently been Steinbrenner; the reporter hadn't talked to Torborg), was even less amused by Martin's comment. But Ellis let it roll off him, and in a bit of pregame needling with Shane Rawley prior to the season's final game, told Rawley that if the pitcher wanted help next year, he'd have to find Ellis "with the Cairo Pharoahs over in the Nile Valley League. We've got to wear these funny white robes for uniforms, but the pay's real good."

Surprisingly—and one has to believe that it came as a surprise even to Steinbrenner—the big loser in the aftermath of Fowler's firing was Don Zimmer. Torborg was protected from Martin's wrath by his location in the bullpen, Ellis simply listened to it and laughed, Yogi was Yogi, and by that time, Roy White was so deep in his shell that Martin could have walked across his shoulders in spikes and White would hardly have noticed. Zimmer was as tough as anybody in a Yankee uniform—in this, his tobacco-chewing, ex-Marine image was far from false—but he was genuinely sensitive to Martin's moods and fears. Fully aware that the consensus around the league was that he'd been hired as coach in order to be handy when Steinbrenner did eventually get around to firing Martin, Zimmer punctiliously observed the manager's authority. Known as one of the most astute men in baseball at the delicate art of positioning infielders defensively, Zimmer didn't even begin doing that until Martin asked him. And even then, he rarely moved the players around on his own, merely asking a question—"Is *that* where you want Robertson to play?"— as a nonthreatening way of letting an inattentive or preoccupied Martin know that a player was out of position. Zimmer had been able to carve out this role for himself both because Martin was among those who respected him and because there was no one else on the bench who had any particular claim to expertise in that area. After about two months of such exchanges, Zimmer had quietly begun to move into Martin's inner circle, and by the time Fowler was fired, it was not at all unusual to find Zimmer and Martin together in the manager's office, going over scouting reports or, increasingly, just talking.

But all those gradual developments, though obviously of benefit to the Yankees, came to a sudden halt with Fowler's departure. To begin with, and to no one's surprise, Martin withdrew. More seriously, in

< 57 >

the manner of a seigneur delivering a brace of rabbits to a peasant family after crushing their child's legs under his carriage, Steinbrenner responded to the American League's de facto exoneration of Martin by allowing him to hire yet another designated confidant. Martin chose Lee Walls.

During a major league career that had ended in 1964, Walls had been a competent, though not particularly distinguished, outfielder. He'd batted above .300 once (.304 with Chicago in 1958, when he'd also hit 24 home runs), but during the last five years of his career he'd never played more than 100 games a season, had hit more than .270 only once, and had averaged only three home runs a year. He'd always been considered an above-average defensive player, primarily because he compensated for his lack of speed by playing the hitters intelligently. A long-time California resident, and a veteran of the old Hollywood Stars of the Pacific Coast League, Walls had been a holdover coach at Oakland when Martin arrived there for the 1980 season.

Walls was in some ways an even greater contrast to Martin than Fowler had been—at four or five inches taller than the manager, with a shining shaven head, Walls had a taste for elegant clothes that he exercised on the team's nights off—but the two got along, and Walls had stayed at Oakland through Martin's tenure. When Martin rejoined the Yankees, Walls came to spring training with him. There, his duties consisted primarily of hitting pregame fly balls for the outfielders to shag. But when he entered the dugout after Fowler's firing, he began to take a somewhat more aggressive role. Appearing with a white towel draped about his neck, Walls used the easily visible towel to move the outfielders around, waving it like a semaphore flag to attract their attention.

Though Walls inherited Fowler's locker—the one nearest the manager's office—and filled, to a great degree, Fowler's role as Martin's bar partner, his relationship with Martin was of a different caliber than Fowler's had been. Fowler had unhesitatingly described Martin as the best manager he'd ever seen, but he also felt free, in private, to question and challenge the manager's decisions. Over the years, he'd learned when and how to accomplish this without provoking a Martin outburst, and Martin was the first to admit that in some of their late-night conversations Fowler's arguments convinced him.

Walls perhaps lacked the skills to pull off that part of Fowler's role,

< 58 >

and certainly lacked the inclination. More given to hero worship, he was content—even eager—to be a yes man. Sometimes the effect was a little unsettling. In a game against Chicago, for instance, Martin—who regularly received signals from his catcher about whether or not each pitch was in the strike zone—was getting on umpire Dale Ford. Walls, with perhaps a two-beat pause, repeated—virtually word for word—the manager's routinely obscene criticisms, and at one point the umpire walked over to the Yankee bench and announced, "I'll take it from you, Billy, but not from Lee Walls." It was after this incident that the players derisively began to call Walls "Echo." Indeed, he echoed Martin's opinions, sometimes in Martin's words, so thoroughly that Walls—six feet three inches and described by the Yankee press office as "nondescript American"—once astounded reporters in the Chicago hotel bar by referring to himself as "a tough little Dago."

Walls did, however, feel free to act on his own in setting outfield defenses, and one day soon after his arrival he began moving infielders around as well. This was almost certainly not an attempt to supplant Zimmer—Walls's ambitions were limited to pleasing Martin—but rather a failure to realize that the manager, still in a funk over Fowler, had pulled back from communicating with *all* his coaches and that what appeared to be a dangerous vacuum was merely a combination of Martin's depression and Zimmer's hesitation to tread on it. But on the day that Walls began to whirl his towel around and shout "Hey, Andre," toward the shortstop's slot, Zimmer headed down to the water-cooler end of the dugout. Prideful himself, Zimmer stayed there for what one player called "a two-month drink of water," while he waited for Martin to call him back.

Eventually, Martin did, but not before considerable damage had been done to the Yankees. The veteran infielders—Nettles, Smalley, Randolph—could pretty much position themselves. They were familiar with the opposing batters and had a good sense of the way various Yankee pitchers' balls behaved. But Andre Robertson, the rookie whose increasingly regular play at shortstop coincided with the team's resurgence from their terrible start, needed help from the bench, and Walls was simply not as good as Zimmer. In the first forty-four games he played, when Fowler had been around and Zimmer was taking an active role, Robertson committed only four errors; in the remaining

< 59 >

fifty-four before his injury, he made eleven, more than doubling his rate. And, typically for a rookie, his play in the field spilled over to his performance at the plate. Over those first forty-four games, he batted .265; after that, .236. The combined slippage was serious enough that Martin was forced into benching him for a couple of days. Because he never returned to the team after his automobile accident, there's no way to tell how long the "rest" would have lasted, but as players like Kemp had discovered, it could stretch out interminably.

At about the time he'd had to sit Robertson, Martin realized how seriously the team had missed Zimmer and called him back into the fold. By then, however, Zimmer—in a decision that would wind up affecting Martin directly—had already made up his mind that 1983 was going to be his last year as a Yankee coach.

< 60 >

6

Baseball Rhythms I:
The Mound

Baseball is a symphony of rhythms. A pitcher finds his in the dance of the ball, the off-speed curves away that set up the fastball, the heaters that set up the change; a batter's lies within the coordinated interplay of hips and wrists orchestrated by his eyes. Multiplied, these come together in the rhythm of a game—the procession of half-innings, the ritual preparations of pitcher and batter, even the loosening-up exercises in the on-deck circle. To stand outside a stadium during a game is to hear the fans dancing to the beat. The noise is steadier than football's or tennis's, the crescendos and diminuendos less dramatic, less predictable in their timing. Over a three-hour stretch, there may be but one or two explosions of sound—for a dramatic home run, perhaps, or a key strikeout. More often than not, what one hears is anticipation—handclaps or chants of "We want a hit" building to a shrill scream with the rise of a deep fly ball—and disappointment—the shout settling into a sigh as the ball falls to a waiting fielder. These rhythms, endlessly reiterated over the long season, finally reveal their meaning when July's largo becomes September's allegro.

For all but a few teams, all but a few players, disappointment is the symphony's dominant motif. Waiting behind their pitcher, fielders

< 61 >

want the ball. With each windup, they lean forward, ready to sprint, to dive, to leap. Strikes, balls, and out-of-play fouls are letdowns. And even when the batter makes contact, most of the defenders are spectators whose role—like the bleacherites'—is simply to urge someone else on. Except for the catcher and first baseman, fielders are likely to touch a batted ball no more than five or six times per game—not much more often than they bat.

By an ineluctable law of averages, batting is by definition disappointing. The .300 hitter—someone who fails to get a hit seven out of ten times—is a paradigm of excellence. And even if one counts walks as successes, the failure rate for all but the very best batters exceeds six out of ten. In most other professional sports, any player who even approached such disappointing numbers—a wide receiver who dropped 70 percent of the passes thrown to him, a power forward who averaged only 30 percent from the floor—would soon be dropped from the squad. And though frequent disappointment may be a hallmark of other low-scoring games like hockey or soccer, it's neither as dramatically individual nor as lingering as baseball's. In those games, too much is happening too fast for any player to brood or get caught up in his own misery. Only baseball players, hearing jeers as they stand isolated in the field or sitting on the bench with their faces buried in their hands, are blessed—or cursed—with sufficient time to savor their inadequacies.

They get to do this, with only an occasional day off, for 162 games scheduled during a half-year that marches from cold to warm and back to cold again, and the survivors become at once optimists and fatalists. Though the long season is a physical and emotional grind, it carries within it a thousand chances for redemption, as well as for ignominy. "Wait 'til next year," the fan's article of faith, is simply a player's "We'll get 'em tomorrow" stretched on a longer time-frame.

Thus the game encourages—and, for most players, demands—what at first might appear to be a kind of flatness. In football locker rooms, the pregame air vibrates with tension. Players bang themselves against walls, snarl, and even scream as they prepare to go out and bash their opponents into the ground. In baseball, the locker room feels more like what it has traditionally been called: the clubhouse. The Yankees, for instance, have devoted card players who differ from suburban bridge groups only in the exaggerated physicality with which they

< 62 >

slam their winning trumps on the table. Other young men skim news-papers or labor over crossword puzzles, and many—especially if any sporting event this side of Championship Bowling is scheduled—gather around the television. Don Baylor, endlessly scraping and boning his bats to achieve the elusive balance between body and weightlessness that may let him get around on a pitch a millisecond faster, is one of the few who seem actually to be preparing to play baseball. The deepest intensity comes from Lou Piniella and the other students of horseflesh as they debate the day's racing form.

Only with this kind of shared equanimity—a resignation that comes from the hard-earned realization that today's screaming liner right to the shortstop will be balanced by tomorrow's bloop single—can play-ers weather the game's spiritual and physical debilitations. Until the season's final out—which seems, until it thunders toward the players like a jet cleared for takeoff, unimaginably distant—another chance is as near as your next at bat.

Unless you're a starting pitcher. Not only are the standards of success and failure different—on a winning team, a pitcher with a .500 won-lost percentage is fully as marginal as a .250 hitter—the chances for redemption are further apart. No team uses less than a four-man rotation, and because Guidry and Rawley require four days' rest, the Yankees go with five starters. Batters come to the plate five or six hundred times during the course of a season, but starting pitchers get the chance to prove themselves no more than thirty or so times a year. Within a group whose talents have already separated them from the rest of us, pitchers are a breed apart.

At one time or another in their careers, most professional ballplay-ers were pitchers. Walk onto any sandlot, even any Little League field, and you will see that the outstanding athletes are the shortstop and the pitcher. Somewhere along the line, in college or the low minors, the level of talent around these players rises, and most are converted to other positions. At least some of the pitchers who watch an out-fielder play an out into a double and think "*I* could have caught that" are probably right, but only the most deluded outfielder, watching a ball sail over his head and into the stands, imagines that he could have struck the batter out. Though this disparity of talent—or at least of a certain kind of talent—is generally admitted, most players don't talk about it, except as a kind of joke. "I had a heckuva fastball," says

< 63 >

Dave Winfield, whose 13–1 record during his senior year at the University of Minnesota makes it likely that he *could* have been a pitcher, "I could throw it right through the backstop. *Nobody* wanted to go up there and hit against me. Of course," he adds with a veteran's practiced timing, "there were lots of times I *did* throw it through the backstop instead of over the plate. . . ." Formally unacknowledged, the special status and talent of starting pitchers creates a certain edginess among the players. It would be hard, for instance, to think of two ballplayers whose styles differ as widely as Oscar Gamble's and Willie Randolph's. Gamble is loud, a needler, and a classic slugger and Randolph an introspective slap-hitter, yet on the road they spend hours together. Pitchers, however, tend to hang out with pitchers. Only other pitchers can understand their suffering.

And suffer they do. As pitching coach Sammy Ellis once put it, "A pitcher can be horseshit all by himself, but he can't win a game without help." Arguably more talented than his teammates, a pitcher is nonetheless at their mercy. If they are hitting and fielding well, they can rescue him on one of those inevitable days when he doesn't have his stuff, and even on those days when he approaches perfection, they can fritter away a victory. Though pitchers thus victimized may achieve low e.r.a.'s, they don't win a lot of games; in that sense, one of baseball's traditional benchmarks of superiority, the 20-win season, conspires against pitchers. Batters who do well in a losing cause will see their efforts recognized in virtually every statistic, and though there's probably some marginal difference in the number of good pitches each sees, the best hitter on the last-place club has just about as much chance to win a batting championship as the best hitter on the pennant winner. During the second half of the 1983 season, the Red Sox were the worst team in the division, but no one thinks that batting champ Wade Boggs or home run leader Jim Rice had bad seasons. But what about Shane Rawley, who failed to get a single win in his last six starts and wound up with a mediocre 14–14 record? And what about Dave Righetti?

Rawley first. During the final month of the season, he had one genuinely bad outing, giving up five earned runs in five innings to Cleveland, but his other losses were tough indeed. In the crucial series versus the Orioles at the Stadium, he gave up only two earned runs in eight and a third innings, but absorbed the loss when Baltimore

< 64 >

scored six runs during his ninth-inning shower. Two starts later, he went a full nine innings, holding the Red Sox to three runs; but after Don Baylor hit into a bases-loaded double play to quiet a key threat, the Yankees scored only two. On the final day of the season, he again went all the way, giving the division-champion Orioles only two runs, but the Yankees were shut out. Killing time in a low-stakes poker game on the bus ride home, Rawley seemed superficially in control of himself but would occasionally fail to realize it was his turn to bet, while he muttered the scores of his losing games over and over again in a quiet, desperate mantra.

But by Righetti's standards, Rawley got plenty of support. Through most of the season, Righetti had the best stuff of any Yankee pitcher. Though Kemp and Smalley each made a brilliant play behind him during the course of his Fourth of July no-hitter against the Red Sox, nobody regarded his accomplishment as a fluke. Going into the All-Star break, he was among the league leaders in won-lost percentage, and when his record hit 12–3 he seemed to have the best shot of any Yankee pitcher at a twenty-win season. But after a streak of disasters that might have been laughable had they not been so painful, he finished the season at only 14–8, six short of the magic number. In some of those losses, it appeared that a peculiarly puckish god had spent some time devising new ways to test this twenty-four-year-old's character.

In an all-too-typical game against the White Sox, Righetti gave up a first-inning run on a walk, a questionable balk, a short single, and a sacrifice fly. Over the rest of the game, he gave up four hits, no runs, and struck out eleven. He lost 1–0, with the tying Yankee run at third as the game ended. Five days later, in another pitchers' duel, he pitched eight innings of shutout ball before yielding his third hit, a leadoff triple. Leaving the game in the ninth, he watched Gossage give up a single to break the scoreless tie, and though the Yankees went on to win with two runs in the bottom of the ninth, Gossage, not Righetti, was the winning pitcher.

Next time around, on August 26 in Anaheim, Goose did what he was supposed to. With the Yankees leading 3–2 in the bottom of the ninth and the tying runner at third, Gossage came in to protect Righetti's win with a strikeout and a routine fly. But things were pretty much back to normal by the time of Righetti's next start, five

< 65 >

days later at Oakland. Once again, he was superb, giving up only four hits and striking out ten while throwing a complete game, but the Oakland pitcher was even better, getting Winfield to ground out with the bases loaded in the eighth, and winning 2–0. Over the thirty-four and a third innings Righetti was on the mound during those four games, the Yankees scored precisely three runs for him.

As he watched his chance for 20 wins evaporate, Righetti at first remained philosophical. "Sure, it would be nice to get some runs out there," he said after the Oakland loss, "but what the hell, the guys are trying." Eventually, however, the unending disappointment began to get to him. In his final start of the long road trip, September 6, against the contending Brewers at Milwaukee, Righetti didn't have his over-powering stuff and was sneaking by on changes and curves. Neverthe-less, he held the Brewers to a 3–3 tie going into the bottom of the eighth inning, when the leadoff batter reached first on a bad-hop error past Willie Randolph. After a sacrifice bunt attempt turned into a pop-up, Righetti got Robin Yount to hit a perfect double-play grounder to Bobby Meacham, who had come in at shortstop for defensive purposes. Meacham booted it, managing to get the force out, but leaving the Brewers still alive. Offered the equivalent of five outs by the Yankees' fielding, the extra Brewers batters came through, and after a single and a triple off the tiring Righetti (and a run-scoring wild pitch from reliever George Frazier), Milwaukee won 6–3.

Meacham was apologetic—"That was a for-sure double play. Nice and soft, I had it all the way. No excuses at all."—but Righetti was devastated. Tears shining in his eyes, he slumped in front of his locker and spoke in a bare whisper. After managing to defend his rookie teammate by saying that this wasn't his worst loss, he continued— hesitantly, but without further questions—"They all seem bad. I can't stand to lose." And then, his voice rising, "I just can't fucking stand it. I'm *never* gonna be able to accept it. Sure, it would be nice to have a big lead once in a fucking while, or nice not to have errors, but I want to go out there and be *perfect.*"

He paused, and mustered a half-smile, "I wish I *was* perfect for once, but I guess that's not the way life works, and the sun's still gonna come up tomorrow. . . . I guess."

For Righetti, for any starting pitcher, the notion that a loss is the end of the world is not entirely a joke. The every-fifth-day rhythm

< 66 >

pitchers establish for themselves is closer to professional football's weekly climax than it is to the summer game's quotidian grind, and the baseball truism that pitchers are crazy has less to do with any personal eccentricities than with the fact that they play a different *kind* of baseball from the rest of the team. Though the rhythms of the pitcher's psyche are alien, the other players by and large respect the difference, giving a losing pitcher an hour of brooding (or a night of drinking) before once again including him in the daily needling, and allowing the day's pitcher to go undisturbed through his ritual—Guidry's solitaire, Fontenot's pacing—of pregame concentration.

Perhaps the only exception to that rule during the year came in Righetti's first home start after his no-hitter. As the players drove into the Stadium, they were greeted by the game-day sign reading not "Yankees vs. Texas" but "Righetti vs. Texas." Righetti, concentrated as usual, had noticed the sign—and thought it was "nice"—but hadn't really focused on it. At least not until he looked up from his locker and realized that most of his teammates hadn't yet dressed for batting practice. Puzzled, he asked if something was going on, and was greeted with a chorus of hooting remarks about how he was such a star he was going to play the Rangers all by himself. Picking up one of the wads of tape that had accompanied these comments, a laughing Righetti flung it at his loudest tormentor, Oscar Gamble. He missed, and Gamble continued "Oh, oh. Little Davey hasn't got his control tonight. What's he gonna do if he walks somebody? Not gonna pick him off with nobody playin' first."

Righetti seemed to enjoy the raillery, but after the game, in which he gave up five runs but won, he said, "You like to have fun, sure, like to feel relaxed, but I think I was a little too relaxed out there tonight. Normally I'm pretty quiet on the day I pitch, but the guys had a lot of fun with me tonight. I guess that's inevitable, maybe, but I wish they hadn't. I mean, I'd sure feel terrible if we'd lost this game."

In their self-imposed isolation, and in the intensity their position on the mound imposes on them, starting pitchers can get lonely. Even more than the fact that they can afford to wake with a hangover on one of their off-days, this perhaps accounts for their notorious conviviality at the bar; and if their singular rhythm sometimes sets them apart, the regularity of their schedule offers compensations. Relief

< 67 >

pitchers have the worst of both worlds, especially short relievers, for like a man trying at once to tango and to waltz, they have to combine a starting pitcher's concentration with a regular's ability to avoid highs and lows.

Goose Gossage is perhaps the most ferociously concentrated player in baseball. So intense is his focus on the batter that from time to time, especially if the lead run is on base, Nettles will have to walk over from third to remind Gossage to hold the runner. Though this season was a long way from Gossage's best, he continues to thrive on his job's special pressures. Waiting for the start of a rain-delayed July game, he compared his job with a starter's. "You don't have to do all this *getting ready*," he said. "When you come in and the game is on the line, the situation pumps you up automatically. When I used to start, I hated it. I mean I really *hated* starting—and I didn't feel as a pitcher that I pitched up to my talent in that role, either. Four fuckin' days between starts with nothing to do except sit there and be a cheerleader. . . . Terrible.

"I'll tell you, if I wasn't a baseball player, I'd want to play basketball. That's a great sport. Go, go, go all the time and never sit down. Right now, I love pitching when I'm out there, but even for me—and I pitch a *lot*—the dead time is a killer. It's worst on days when I've like gone three innings the day before, and I know there's no way I'm gonna get in there. Then I get the same feeling of uselessness I did when I was a starter. Otherwise, even if it's kinda boring during the early part of the game, when it gets to be about the sixth inning I can feel the adrenaline starting to flow.

"And it's *gotta* flow, you know? If a hitter's going bad, having a bad couple of days, someone else can pick him up. If I screw up, the headlines say 'Gossage Blows It.' When that happens, and you can be sure it's gonna happen to *everyone,* the worst thing you can do to a pitcher is not put him out there in the same situation the next time. It's like a horse, when you break his spirit.

"It's worse, really, because *you're* thinking, and the horse isn't. You get afraid people have lost confidence in you, afraid you've maybe lost something yourself, so you go out there and try to do too much, start overthrowing. I mean, hell, I always look like I'm overthrowing, because I throw the ball so hard, but I can be really within myself and be throwing ninety-five miles an hour. It's when I get crazy and try

< 68 >

to throw a hundred that I get in trouble."

Though Martin never showed any signs of losing confidence in Gossage, there were a couple of times during the year—especially after games in which he'd given up leads—that Gossage did appear to be trying to throw the ball beyond his limits, but he was often able to reestablish control over himself and salvage the game. Toward the end of July, he ran into a classic bad patch, giving up late-inning leads against Kansas City twice in the four-game series that included George Brett's famous pine-tar homer. Though both of these disasters turned into wins for Gossage and the Yankees (the pine-tar game only temporarily), Goose was plainly bothered by his lack of success.

Typically, however, his job didn't give him much time to brood, and the day after the pine-tar game he was once more on the mound—this time in Arlington, Texas, nursing a 4–2 lead for Righetti in the eighth inning.

After giving up two unearned runs in the second, Righetti had yielded only a walk and a single over the next five innings, but he opened the eighth with a single and a walk, and Gossage came in with the leading run at the plate. He promptly gave up two singles and a sacrifice fly—and the lead. During this nationally televised performance, even viewers who lacked particular skill in lipreading were able to see him walk off the mound and scream to himself "I'm such fucking horseshit" before retiring the inning's final batter.

In the visitor's ninth, however, the Yankees put together two singles, a wild pitch, and a monster Winfield triple into the right-center gap to reclaim the lead at 5–4. Then Gossage went back out and retired the side in order. Afterward, he waxed philosophical: "I got them in New York; they got me here. That's the game. Nobody feels worse than I do about fucking up somebody's 'W'—I've done that to Rags a couple a times this year—but you can't let it get to you. I mean, if I'd been a less experienced pitcher, I'd probably go out there and fuck up the ninth 'cause I was still so pissed off about the eighth. But you can't do that and survive. You've got to stay within yourself out there. You start losing your rhythm, you might as well start getting warmed up for the next old-timers' game."

It's that momentary falter in a pitcher's rhythm that batters thrive on. Talking about the conventional wisdom that hitters prepare for a fastball and adjust to a breaking pitch, Lou Piniella dismissed it as

< 69 >

"true only up to a point. In this league at least, the really successful hitters guess a lot. I know that once I've seen a pitcher three or four times—certainly once I've seen him for three or four games—I have a pretty good idea what he's going to do in certain situations. That's why a batter loves to see the count at two-and-oh or three-and-one. You know the guy out there's gotta throw it over the plate, so you zone the ball: You decide ahead of time where he's gonna put it—low, high, inside, outside—and what kind of pitch he's gonna throw, and you narrow your strike zone to *that* pitch. If it's somewhere else, let it go by; he's still gotta give you one or two more chances to hit the ball. But if it's there, you're *ready* for it. That's when you get your extra-base hits, and that's when you get pitchers in trouble, because once you're on base, he's got to pitch a little differently. He doesn't want the big inning, so he's going to pitch a little more cautiously. What you've done is you've taken some options away, made him a little more predictable, and if he gets behind the *next* batter, then he's really in trouble.

"There are," he continued, "a lot of good pitchers in this league—there aren't any bad ones, that's for sure—but there's only a handful of great ones. Those are the guys who can either challenge you and get away with it—put it right in your zone and *dare* you to hit it—or the ones who consistently outguess you, who *always* have you lookin' at that three-and-one strike. But even with them, you've gotta make your own guess and get ready for a ball in your zone, because once or twice a game, even those guys are gonna lose their rhythm or try to do too much with a ball, and if you're not ready, that's a real lost opportunity. The only real difference between the good pitchers and the great ones is that the great ones don't yield to the situation around them. They're kind of self-contained, and they're gonna make you hit *their* pitch, not yours."

On the face of it, Gossage seems an unlikely candidate for staying within himself. A physically intimidating presence—at six feet three inches and 215 pounds, he's one of the few Yankees able to stand next to Winfield without somehow appearing smaller than he actually is —his fits of temper sometimes unsettle even his teammates. In one of this year's games, when Nettles had come toward the mound to remind him that the runner on second was a threat to steal, Gossage's "Get the fuck outta here" was audible in the nearby box seats. And,

< 70 >

of course, he was disabled for ten weeks during the 1979 season after injuring his thumb in a locker-room fight with Cliff Johnson, then a Yankee.

Johnson, now Toronto's designated hitter, was fully Gossage's size, but when the Goose's anger takes hold, he strikes without fear or favor. Many reporters treasure copies of a classic 1982 Gossage tirade during which he scornfully refers to Steinbrenner as "the fat man," and this year—riding back to the hotel after a tough loss to the California Angels—he attacked the media in a ten-minute diatribe that began "Greasy fuckin' cocksuckers" and built up from there. Even within a profession not known for gentility, Gossage is remarkably crude. His most frequent reading matter, to which he gives detailed attention, are skin magazines of the most graphic sort. Occasionally, he carries one or two into his pregame whirlpool, and has been known to sign autographs for children while resting their slips of paper on top of a wide-open magazine.

After all this, mentioning that Gossage is deeply concerned about —and seems more than passingly attentive to—his own children might seem a little like pointing out that Hitler was fond of dogs, but there really are a handful of different Gossages that need appraisal before one can take his measure. Much of what appears to be crudity or insensitivity is really no more than a sort of bearish clumsiness, for despite experiencing a near-constant stream of media attention since he came to the Yankees as a free agent in 1978, Gossage remains very much a country boy. Deeply private, and in a curious way shy, he is a throwback to an earlier baseball era.

Raised in the mountains outside Colorado Springs, Gossage—like many American boys—dreamed of being a big league ballplayer. A local high school star, he knew just enough to know how little that was: "I knew I could get guys out in Colorado Springs, but that doesn't tell you a whole lot. The funny thing is that my father, he always used to tell people I was going to pitch in the big leagues.

"I was from a relatively poor family—not dirt poor, or anything, but we didn't have a whole lot of material things. I used to spend a lot of time with my father, though. He was a landscaper, or was supposed to be, but that didn't really work out, because he would rather have been hunting or fishing, and a lot of the time he was. He was my big booster, though, and once I started out, my mom was a

< 71 >

hundred percent behind me too. She used to come to all the games, cheer, make special dinners and all that. But actually being in the big leagues, that was like a dream."

In 1970, when Gossage graduated from high school, he was drafted by the Chicago White Sox organization. And he was frightened: "I was thinking, then, I should get my college. And I think that's sort of right for most people, but I know guys who went through eight years of school to do something they don't want to do. So I must have talked to *everybody* about the White Sox offer: 'What should I do? What should I do?' A couple of them tossed it back to me—'What do you *want* to do?'—and when they put it that way, what I wanted to do was pitch in the major leagues. But when I finally signed it, I was so scared I went home and cried. I got in my brother's jeep and drove up to the hills out by the Springs there and just kind of sat there by myself wondering if I'd done the right thing.

"You see, there was nobody there to tell me what it was like. All I knew, I got from television baseball—Dizzy Dean and Pee Wee Reese once a week. And I was thinking, there goes my college, there goes being a forest ranger, but by then it was too late."

Naive and nervous, Gossage was assigned to the White Sox's Rookie League team in Sarasota. "I'd never been out of Colorado, never even been on an airplane, but I got this big stack of directions and had to go to Tampa, Florida. This was June, maybe July, and when I got off the plane, I felt heat like I'd never felt before. It was like a hundred degrees and a hundred degrees humidity. You had to push through it. It was like walking into a wall, right, so I asked somebody if it was the heat from the jet exhaust, and he just laughed and said, 'Welcome to Florida.' "

This was only the first of several unpleasant surprises awaiting the rookie. On the instructions he'd been given, it said he should go to the limousine that would be waiting there. "I figured, great, you know, I'm a ballplayer and I'm going to ride a big black limo, so I walked out, kinda doing my best to look like a guy who did this every day, and asked where my limo was. The guy said, 'Where you goin'?' and when I told him the Sarasota Motor Hotel, he just pointed. And it wasn't a limousine, man, I'll tell you that. It was a van full of people, and it must've stopped everywhere between Tampa and Sarasota. It would drive down little streets and drop you right at your house, you

< 72 >

know. And it's dark, and I can't see anything, and I don't have any idea where I am, and I was the last one off. It must've been about three or four in the morning and I had to bang on the door of the office for about twenty minutes before somebody let me in. I'm just standing out there in the parking lot with my suitcases, bangin' on this door, and I'm thinking 'This is it? This is the big leagues?' "

At that point, Gossage was the classic hard-throwing rookie—"I had something I thought was a breaking ball, but it was more like a pitch that you just throw up there"—but he was good enough to overpower other rookies who were probably just as scared as he was, and in one appearance he struck out nine of the twelve batters he faced. After three games, the White Sox had seen enough, and sent Gossage north to the Appleton, Wisconsin, Foxes in the A League. "I was oh-and-three and got my ass kicked all the time. Really gettin' my ass kicked, you know. I think it was just my head was spinning. I was eighteen years old, homesick, and I wasn't used to the lack of privacy. I mean, I had a lot of friends when I was growing up, but I was always solitary, too. I used to get off by myself in the woods, not talking to anyone, for a whole day. There was no way of doing that in Appleton, and I kept on hearing that the manager there wanted to release me. I got home that winter not knowing what I was going to do, and I got a job humping furniture in a moving and storage company. I'm there trying to jam somebody's couch through the front door and I'm thinking, "I coulda been in *college,* man.' "

But he went back to Appleton, which didn't seem as strange the second time around, where he was 18–2, leading the league in earned-run average, complete games, and shutouts. He had only one more winter of moving furniture for a living. In 1972, the White Sox invited him to spring training as a nonroster player, and he stuck with them, skipping Double-A and Triple-A ball. "Johnny Sain taught me the breaking ball I have now," he says, "more of a 'slurve' instead of just a little slider or a big curve, and that just set me up. I had two pitches now, but that made me *four* times the pitcher I used to be." He had a couple of trips back to the minors during the next two seasons, "but when I look back on that first decision—should I sign this contract? —there's not a thing I'd change."

But the success, especially success in the short-reliever's spot, hasn't come without cost. "I feel like baseball's hardened me a lot.

< 73 >

Like sometimes toward the press, you know. A lot of these guys, it's just, blame, blame, blame. And I don't need that. There's nobody feels fuckin' worse than I do when I lose a game.

"And let me tell you, *I'm* the one who loses them. Every now and then, maybe once or twice a season, a fielder'll make a terrible play, or a guy will do something stupid on the bases. They're like in shell shock, man. They sit there and say 'I lost a ball game.' That happens to me *every* time we lose. I can handle defeat—I can get it out of my body somehow—but I can't handle all the negativity.

"I'll tell you, I used to be a lot nicer than I am. Now, I'll be walking out to the bullpen, and somebody yells 'Hey, Gossage, you fuckin' stink,' and I'll just say, 'Hey, fuck you.' Before, it would've hurt my feelings.

"And I still have feelings. After that Brett home run in the playoffs, I cried. I felt like I let a lot of people down. I was in the players' lounge in the Stadium, in front of all my friends, and I was just crying like a baby. I guess that really hasn't changed too much; I did the same thing in high school when I lost a playoff game in Legion ball.

"But you can't do that every day and survive. You have to harden up, especially on this team, where there's always somebody a half an inch behind your ass waiting to bite it." For a moment, he veered away from the subject of rhythm to the topic that had been occupying him more and more as the season progressed. "You know, it's not *fun* playing baseball here. It hasn't *been* fun since the 1981 Series, when George made that damn apology. There we were in a fuckin' World Series, man, supposed to be the greatest time in your life, and George is acting like we did something shameful. We're the American League champions, and George is all over the television talking like we were a fuckin' bunch of criminals. He's a good owner in a lot of ways—he really cares about this team—but sometimes he just doesn't know shit. I've had days this year, for the first time in my whole fuckin' life, when I've looked at the clock and said 'Oh, shit. It's time to go to the ballpark.' That's a *terrible* feeling to have. This is supposed to be a *game* we're playing, I shouldn't feel like I'm on my way in to punch a clock in a factory."

Long before the arrival of Steinbrenner, the Yankees seemed to have less fun playing ball than some of their famous rivals—St. Louis's Gas House Gang or Brooklyn's scrappy Boys of Summer. But

< 74 >

that Yankee aura had been cooly aristocratic; they were professionals, and the other guys were just playing a game. Despite the fact that he'd made them wealthier, Steinbrenner had in many ways turned the Yankees from lords to laborers. The old Yankee teams had seemed accountable only to themselves; the 1983 players were being watched, measured, criticized, and even derided by the Boss.

Except in his role as lightning rod for the owner's anger, Martin didn't provide Gossage or any of the Yankees with much relief, for in his own way he was as driven and quick to blame as Steinbrenner. Someone was indeed always half an inch behind the players' asses, and many of them kept nervously waiting for the jaws to snap. Gossage, who maintained much of childhood's emotionalism, might not have been entirely comfortable on those earlier Yankee teams, but he was miserable in the judgmental joylessness of the 1983 clubhouse. For him, actually getting on the mound was a release. "Sometimes, after a bad loss, I'm *amazed* that I can go out there the next day and do anything at all. But fortunately," he grinned, "there's this gorilla in me that just takes over.

"Of course," he added, returning to the subject of rhythm, "when it does, somebody's gotta keep it on a leash. I don't care how fast your throw; if you throw nothing but fastballs, there are hitters in this league that are gonna catch up to you. Someone's gotta slow me down.

"But that's hard for a catcher to do. If I'm gonna get beat, I want to get beat on my best pitch, not on some off-speed thing that's just supposed to set the fastball up. But what happens is, I get out there, and I throw a ball at ninety-five miles an hour easy, so I just gather up my strength and try humming the sombitch at a hundred. I'm out there, and I feel that with just a little more effort, I could throw the sucker right through the catcher—and maybe halfway through the umpire, too.

"The thing is, it doesn't go as fast, 'cause my asshole's tight. It's pretty hard to throw a ball with one hand around your throat. And when that happens, even before everybody's turning around to watch the fuckin' home run, it affects the team. It's like your kids; when they see fear in your face, they get afraid too, even if they don't know why. In the clubhouse or at the hotel, everybody's got his own personality. But when I'm out there with runners on second and third, one out, and a one-run lead, *I'm* responsible for the whole team."

< 75 >

But just as Gossage is a major league pitcher, he's facing major league hitters. Even if he feels no fear, even if he finds his perfect rhythm, he's going to blow a few. "The only thing about that is you can't take it home with you. It's not like I'm a starter and I have to think about it for five days, have to spend my time saying 'Damn, that was a stupid pitch.' Except for the playoffs or the Series, there's *always* tomorrow. You know, it's like hunting. 'Some days you eat the bear, some days the bear eats you.' "

< 76 >

7

Baseball Rhythms II:
The Batter's Box

Hitters, like pitchers, have their own distinctive rhythms. These are of two sorts as well: the individual set of movements and strategies contained in a single swing or a single at bat, and the streaks and adjustments that fill the long season. For the 1983 Yankees, no players more clearly indicated the central importance of these rhythms than Don Baylor and Steve Kemp.

There were similarities between the two: both were born in Texas, both came to the Yankees as free agents after New York's disastrous 1982 season—a fact which made both of them young millionaires— and both were supposed to turn the team around. They even rode to the Stadium together when the Yankees were at home. But there were differences as well, differences beyond the fact that Steve Kemp's disappointing season almost ended in tragedy and that Don Baylor's was a striking success. The most obvious was that Baylor was black, Kemp white; though it was only the most obvious, not necessarily the most telling, it's where Baylor's story began.

Seated in front of his locker in the Tigers' jammed-together visitors' clubhouse, Baylor traced a small circle on his left thigh, then quickly surrounded it with a larger one. Stabbing his finger into the center of the doughnut he'd described on the leg of his quilted long johns, he

< 77 >

said, "That's where I grew up. West Austin, one of the oldest black communities around." It was there, in 1964, that thirteen-year-old Don Baylor first made history; in the fall of 1964, he and two other West Austin classmates integrated the Austin school system. "The large black community was way over in East Austin," he said, "and for years, people had been bused over there to the all-black schools. But that fall, for the first time, we were given a choice, and my parents just thought I should go to the nearest school, which was O. Henry Junior High."

Baylor's parents, like most of West Austin's black families, were models of stable, middle-class achievement. A century earlier, with the end of slavery, West Austin had become home for the maids and butlers who served the surrounding white community, and it remained a solid, bourgeois enclave distinct from the more raucous area east of the city, where many of the field-workers had settled. Baylor's father was a blue-collar worker in the baggage service of the Southern Pacific Railroad, the nearest equivalent to civil service employment available to most black southerners, and his mother worked as a dietitian in the Austin school system. As someone who handled food and not students, she was allowed to function in the kitchens of the white schools. "My parents, especially my mother, kept me from hanging around with what they call the riff-raff kids," said Baylor, "the kind that would be skipping school. I wouldn't have dared to skip school, because there was my mother right in the school system and she would have heard about it in a minute."

It is hard to overstate the propriety of the black bourgeoisie during those last years of formal, legal segregation. Soft speech, good manners, and neat dress mattered enormously, and if the embrace of propriety sometimes seemed to border on parody as black coeds Scarlett O'Hara'd through the summer heat carrying parasols that complemented their pastel dresses, those early lessons provided Baylor with a dignified equanimity that has proved useful at several stages in his baseball career. "I knew I was always being looked at," he said, "you know, always being evaluated. There were little things—always being the last one to get a football uniform, for instance—that reminded you that you were different."

There were larger problems as well; after Baylor went on to Austin High ("It was a drumroll away from our house. On Friday nights

< 78 >

growing up, I could hear the fight song."), he ran afoul of the South's deepest fear. "You know how it is when you play football, and you kind of get involved with the cheerleaders. They carry signs for you and everything. . . . Now there weren't any of the white cheerleaders carrying signs for me—there was no way they would dare to do that —but there were one or two who would sometimes walk to class with me. That's all it was, really, but I think some of the teachers—and certainly some of the coaches—thought it was more than that. I was called in and told I'd better watch myself, and my mother was given a warning about it too. The girls were good about it—they told the principal they were in high school now, not junior high—but I kind of lost my interest in playing football."

He didn't drop the sport altogether—on the basis of two-way play as wide receiver and cornerback that earned him all-state honors, he was offered a football scholarship to the University of Texas—but he concentrated on baseball, where the coach's neck didn't seem quite so red. "Even with the problems, I might have stayed with football and gone to UT, but Darrell Royal wanted his football players to be only football players," and by then Baylor's baseball abilities had started to attract the attention of major league scouts. "I liked football," he recalled, "basketball too, but I was really getting interested in baseball. That was kind of funny, too, because by then some of the kids that had grown up in East Austin, they came over to Austin High too, and they kept on saying, 'What you doing playing baseball. *We* don't play baseball.' " But Baylor, who laughingly admits that the East Austin kids were supposed to be "tougher," had learned to make his own choices, and shortly after graduating from high school in 1967 he signed a contract with the Baltimore Orioles.

Baylor's progress to the major leagues was steady but slow. Perhaps because he hadn't played college baseball, the conservative Orioles gave him two full seasons in Triple-A before putting him on their twenty-five-man major league roster in 1972. At the start of spring training in 1976, he was sent to Oakland in the trade that brought Reggie Jackson to Baltimore. After a year of enduring Charles Finley, Baylor opted for free agency and joined the California Angels. Though the Angels have had mixed success with their free-agent signings, Baylor clearly earned his keep. During his 1979 MVP year, he played in 162 games, batted .296 with 36 home runs, and piled up

< 79 >

139 r.b.i.'s. In 1982, the final year of his California contract, the overall numbers were less spectacular, but he nonetheless hit a total of 22 game-winning r.b.i.'s, 16 in the sixth inning or later.

Though Baylor was obviously one of the most attractive of the free agents who became available after the 1982 season, it was something of a surprise when the Yankees signed him. The early-season overcrowding made life difficult for the outfielders/dh's—and for Martin, a firm believer in the efficacy of platooning. When Baylor was asked to sit against right-handers to make room for Oscar Gamble, he didn't hesitate to complain to the manager—nor, when asked by reporters, did he deny his complaints. But as Baylor put it after the Yankees swept a late July series against the Rangers in Texas, "We got past that part. This team became a team." The secret, he said, was winning: "No matter what lineup we play, we're always going to have guys sitting on the bench who want to play—and who would be playing with almost any other club. But when we started to win, they couldn't get back into the lineup, because the guys who were out there were doing the job. At that point, it becomes 'Don't rock the boat, we got a good thing going.' If you're losing, it's 'Play me or trade me,' but now, who can complain? I'm pulling for Oscar when he's out there, and he's pulling for me."

One problem facing the Yankee manager in making out his lineup card was that Baylor was pretty much limited to the dh role. This was less a problem of age—at thirty-four, with speed that made him the Yankees' second leading base-stealer, Baylor was surely not too old for the outfield—than of decisions made a couple of seasons earlier in California, decisions about which the prideful Baylor is still bitter. "There's all this 'We're trying to win' talk out there," he said. "Bull *shit,* they're trying to win. Called a kid up from Triple-A—the year before he was playing A ball—and made me into a dh. It was one thing with a player like Joe Rudi," who came to the Angels with Baylor as a free agent. "No one played left field the way he did. Okay, I'll take a back seat and play right, but when he got hurt I was ready to go back to left. Instead, you've got Dave Garcia, who's 'knowledgeable' about baseball, and a front office that keeps saying they want to win, deciding that I can't play the field anymore. I played every day for Earl Weaver—and this was when they had the dh—and I could do that now if it would help the team."

< 80 >

Baylor made a few outfield appearances for the Yankees during the year, but they were rather more of an adventure than either he or the team might have wished. In Toronto, on August 4, when Oscar Gamble's shoulder limited him to dh-ing, Baylor was in left; on the first Toronto fly ball, he nearly crashed into Dave Winfield, who was playing center that night, and two innings later, worried about a high bounce off the artificial surface, Baylor made a very hesitant charge of Lloyd Moseby's looper, letting it fall for an r.b.i. single. "That was Toronto," he said, "and I know I looked uncomfortable out there. But I don't even think the guys from *Toronto* like to play in Toronto."

He would have liked to get more outfield play in hospitable stadiums, however, for he found the dh role especially frustrating on the road. "When I'm not playing in the field," he said, "the biggest problem is that I've got so much excess energy to release. I mean, if you're dh and you ground out with the bases loaded, there's nothing you can do about it. At home, we have a workout room, I'll go up and ride the stationary bicycle. There's a radio, so I can listen to the game and stay in it, and I'll pump for maybe five or ten minutes at a time, maybe twenty to forty minutes a game. But it's very tough on the road. Oakland has a Nautilus so you can go in and stretch a little, but in most places there's nothing. Here," he said, looking around the oversized closet that serves visitors to Tiger Stadium, "it's almost ridiculous. This year, at least, they've put down carpet. There's a hardwood floor underneath it, and last year, you'd come back here to swing a lead bat, and even when you wrapped towels around your spikes you couldn't get any traction. With the carpet, at least you can swing without worrying about falling down. But there's still no way you can build up or taper down; it's swing and sit down, swing and sit down. I kind of become a faucet. It's turn on the concentration— What is this guy pitching? Can I drive in a run? Steal a base? Score? —then shut it down. And what you've got to do—especially if you haven't been able to do much except sit there, so you're ready to burst when you finally get up—is stay within yourself, not overswing, be relaxed." He paused, then added, "All that early stuff, back in Austin, I'd be lying if I said that didn't help. It makes you a tougher individual, the kind of professional player who can handle the good and the bad, no matter how many people are watching you."

•   •   •

< 81 >

As the opposing pitcher set, Baylor stood upright and nearly motionless, a slight flexing of his wrists making the tip of his perpendicular bat cut tiny circles in the air. But nothing about Steve Kemp seemed at ease. He dug in, moved out, kicked dirt, dug in again. In a semicrouch, with the bat angled slightly forward, he jerked his hands up and down, twitching like a galvanized frog. And when he made contact—even an infield pop—he raced toward first as though he wanted to make Charlie Hustle look like George Dog. Kemp was the classic "gives you 110 percent" player, which is fair enough, for over the years the game has given a lot to him.

Kemp's family left Texas for California when he was still a toddler, settling in green comfort near Pasadena, but his childhood idyll was shattered when he was seven years old. "That was when my parents broke up," he said, "and for years, my mom really had to struggle. I don't know how you would have classified us in economic terms before that, but after the divorce we were sort of lower middle class at best. My mom worked as a bookkeeper, and I think things were really rough for my brother, who was only one or two years old. I could do a little more on my own by then, and I knew my own mind. I was really into sports and—it was warm all year there—I must have played baseball every afternoon."

Economically, things eased when Kemp's mother remarried. "I don't want to imply that she hadn't been doing better financially," he said, "but it was sort of an overnight transition back to being upper middle class. There were other problems, though. I was twelve years old then, right on the edge of adolescence, and I think my stepfather and I had a tough adjustment to make. I know *I* did," he added, "and if anything, I probably spent even more time playing baseball after she remarried. I sometimes wish that when my brother got to be twelve or thirteen, I'd been available to him so that he could have had someone to talk to. But I was in college then, playing for USC, and I really wasn't around home that much."

No matter how much time he'd spent playing, and no matter what emotional resonance the game had for him, the scouts didn't think Kemp was a major league prospect. He wasn't drafted after high school, and though he'd received offers of financial aid from a few small colleges, USC didn't offer him even a partial scholarship. "They said they had none available," he recalled, "but if I came on my own

< 82 >

and proved myself, they could give me a partial the next year. I had all the confidence in the world then, and my parents said they'd pay for a year, which turned out real well, because after a year, USC gave me a full ride instead of a partial."

Even then, however, his college coaches didn't trust him in the field, and used him as a dh exclusively. After he made it clear that he'd transfer rather than spend another year dh-ing—"I told them I was never going to play major league ball that way"—they tried him in the outfield. He was no Tony Armas, but he had gained credibility, and was drafted into the Detroit organization after his junior year.

He was still not a complete outfielder, and his former Detroit manager, Ralph Houk, recalls, "I didn't *want* to play him, but he *made* me do it. I can't remember—certainly not in this generation of ballplayers—anyone who ever worked harder to improve himself. He did all right for us, really better than he should have just on ability." And play he did. In 1982, after a trade to the White Sox, Kemp appeared in 160 games, batted .286 (a point over his career average), hit 19 home runs, and had 98 r.b.i.'s. When his 1983 season ended abruptly, on September 8, when he was blindsided by a line drive during batting practice, Kemp was at only .241 with 12 home runs and 49 r.b.i.'s. More seriously, from his point of view, he'd already sat out 28 of the team's 137 games and had in effect been benched for Mattingly.

The benching process had been gradual—a "resting" that simply extended itself—but unmistakable, and by mid-August Kemp was plainly adrift. When the popular Dave LaRoche rejoined the team in Detroit, on August 12, the clubhouse was alive with laughter and greetings, but things were considerably quieter around Kemp's locker. On that day, the *Detroit News* had featured a Jerry Green column saying that "Steve Kemp is ticked off. He has become an irregular with the Yankees and Steve finds it peculiar that his manager rarely talks to him." Some of the quotes—though perfectly plausible—sounded uncharacteristically petulant, but Kemp said he was fairly represented: "There were a couple of reporters who knew me here, knew I was used to playing regularly, and figured they might have a story if they talked to me. I didn't go looking for them" (in fact, I heard him telling Green, "I don't think I'm any kind of story at all for you") "but I'm not going to dodge any questions if somebody asks

< 83 >

them. I wasn't trying to rock the boat or cause problems, because I took—I take—the responsibility for where I'm at."

The question, of course, is, how do you get out of a slump if you don't get playing time? For the first time this season, Kemp sounded defeatist: "That's probably why I'm not going to come out of it. And if I do, it'll just be because I happen to get into a game and get lucky and they keep me playing. There is an abundance of talent here . . . and right now, not playing every day, it's like a progressive thing, like a snowball, it just gets bigger and bigger every time you roll it. You feel the pressure of trying to do well, so you don't, and that increases the pressure the next time. . . .

"I'm certainly not content sitting on the bench. I don't care about the money, the security—I've got a lot of pride, and if I keep going the way I did the first six years of my career, I've got a chance to put some pretty good numbers on the board. But what I said in that article is basically how I feel. I want to be in New York, I'm happy to be in New York, the media has been fair, the fans have been fair. I go out and play as hard as I can, and I know that's appreciated."

How did he explain the nose dive? Did he feel pressure from the fans? From those big contract numbers? "I think it would have showed up right away if I was—but I had a great spring, led the club in hits, home runs, r.b.i.'s. The only thing I can attribute it to is the injury," a bone chip in his shoulder caused by an early season collision with Willie Randolph, "and that's not an excuse, because I *chose* to play. I could have sat down. But all of a sudden after six years and a great spring, it all changed after the injury. Maybe in my mind I was thinking a manager wants the kind of player who can play hurt, or maybe even that people would be criticizing me if I sat right after signing the big contract. But as it turned out, that was the wrong decision. I do feel that Billy has lost confidence in me, I don't think he accepts me as the player he thought I was. Put that along with not playing every day, it all has the snowball effect."

Did Billy have any reaction to the article? "Not really, I just went in yesterday and told him I had talked to some of the reporters and wanted him to hear it first from me. He just said thanks. But I don't think I said anything that's going to hurt this team. I feel I'm part of this ball club and want to do whatever I can to help it. Maybe on other teams I've played on, teams that didn't have the talent this one

< 84 >

has, I've always known the manager's going to stick with me and I'll hang on and eventually come right. The most that happened is you move up or down in the batting order, but you still play. Here, there's always someone ready to take your place. Maybe it's a player who's been hitting well but in another position that's just as overcrowded as the outfield is, or maybe it's someone who's been sitting because he went through a slump and you got his playing time. A manager doesn't really have any choice but to play those guys. Especially on this team—with someone looking over his shoulder all the time, he's got to think about his own job—and especially when we're in a pennant race."

Typically, though, Kemp never stopped working. On those increasingly frequent nights when he wasn't in the starting lineup, he'd hit live pitching early, then go to the outfield to run beside the pitchers. When the Yankees made way for the visiting team, he'd go to the batting cage under the stands and hit for perhaps another half-hour. As the Yankees prepared to finish the pine-tar game, he sounded almost as though he was beginning to regain some of his lost confidence. "What I've been doing is dropping my hands a little—a lot, really, bringing them down almost to my waist. It means instead of pumping down and then up before I swing, I just come up. I've felt awkward doing it, been very self-conscious. Certainly it's the first time in my career I've done anything this radical to my swing, I've always just gone up and hit the ball. But last night was the first time I've felt comfortable with my hands lower. I didn't get any hits"—the center fielder made a nice grab on a deep fly, and a liner to right went as a two-base error—"but I was hitting the ball solid. I think it's starting to come back now, and I think I'm going to be able to help this team —if I can play."

He didn't get the chance. Mattingly continued to start during the entire West Coast trip preceding the September Baltimore series, and by the time the rookie's bat had begun to cool off to the point where Kemp would surely have been restored to the lineup (Mattingly, who finished the month of August at .330, batted .191 for the remainder of the season), he was recovering from postaccident surgery. There's no guarantee that his new swing would have improved matters much, however, for as ugly and unorthodox as his herky-jerky motion had

< 85 >

been, it had served him very well indeed during six years of major league baseball. Abandoning it, turning away from the batting rhythm that had made him a million-dollar ballplayer, looked an awful lot like a panic reaction to the disruption of the psychological rhythm he'd grown accustomed to as a steady starter.

Though Martin can hardly be blamed for Kemp's early-season failures at the plate, the unsettling effects of the benching must be laid at his door, for he did nothing to cushion the blow. Perhaps the manager was simply lulled into passivity by a misreading of Kemp's continued hustle and avoidance of high-volume complaint, but that *Detroit News* column carried an astonishing and accurate quote from Martin: "I don't talk to any of my players. I don't believe in talking to my players when they're in a slump, and I don't believe in talking to my players when they're hitting." Though Martin made exceptions for certain players he's known for years—Nettles, for example—players who needed emotional support weren't going to get it from Martin.

Even leaving Martin's personality aside, free-agent transfer to the Yankees has never come easy. Dave Winfield had an agonizingly slow start his first pinstripe year, and Ken Griffey, the '83 Yankees' leading hitter, struggled through most of 1982. Baylor did well, but he'd been through a similar experience before (in his first year in California, he batted only .251), and his personality helped. Perhaps the roots of his success—and even of Kemp's failure—lay beyond the manager's reach, somewhere on the ballfields of their youths. Though no one who'd ever seen Baylor take out a second baseman during a double-play attempt will argue that he played with less intensity than Kemp, he could indeed turn it on and off like a faucet. Baylor learned the central importance of self-control early, but at the age when newspapers and television cameras were watching young Don Baylor learn that baseball was a long way from the most important thing in life, Kemp was learning just the opposite. Alone, with no reporters present, the game was becoming his father.

< 86 >

8

Sticky Business

Even now, I look at my scorebook for July 24 with a certain sense of wonder. It just doesn't make any sense. The card shows the Yankees ahead 4–3 going into the ninth inning of a Sunday afternoon game against Kansas City. Dale Murray, who was on in relief, had retired six batters in a row, and also got the first two batters in the ninth— a routine 6–3 grounder and a full-count liner that Griffey, leaping, just stabbed. Moving quickly to an 0–2 count on U. L. Washington, Murray was within a pitch of victory, but Washington slapped the ball on the ground past short for a single, and with George Brett coming up, Martin went to his bullpen for Gossage. With a one-strike count, Brett got all the way around on a Gossage fastball and drove it—deep, according both to the scorebook and my memory—over the right-center wall, to give the Royals a 5–4 lead. But there, against all logic, the game ends. Coming off the diamond-shaped mark I use for home runs is an unfamiliar symbol, something like the balloons cartoonists use to indicate speech. On my scorebook, the home run is saying "Pinetar Out!!?"

George Brett was at least as astonished—and considerably more dis-pleased—than I. When plate umpire Tim McClelland finally con-

< 87 >

cluded the lengthy summit conference that had delayed the game for almost ten minutes after the home run and gave the "out" sign in front of the Kansas City bench, Brett erupted from the dugout and charged him. Tobacco spittle flying from his mouth, Brett clearly didn't have reasoned discussion on his mind, and even after a flying tackle by umpire Joe Brinkman slowed him down, it took two umpires and a Kansas City coach to wrestle him away from McClelland. After a comic-opera scene which starred aging reliever Gaylord Perry attempting to grab the bat and hide it only to be chased down in the runway by plainclothes Stadium guards, the field was finally cleared.

In the clubhouse, Brett was calmer, but still angry. "I'm not *saying* it was an illegal bat," he explained, "but it's *possible* the pine tar might have been up as high as the label," that is to say, well beyond the eighteen-inch length the rules permit. "I don't use batting gloves—I don't like the way they feel and I think I hit better without 'em—so I sometimes use a little extra pine tar. But there's no way that ball was anywhere *near* the tar. You hit the ball off the handle, it's gonna be a dink, right? That wasn't a dink. I hit that ball solid, maybe five inches from the end. That's twenty-nine, twenty-nine and a half inches up, and there's no pine tar up that far. Shit, if I ever got jammed and hit the ball *that* far, I'd have seventy-five home runs a year. . . ."

Next door, in the manager's office, Dick Howser was, if possible, even angrier. "To take that kind of home run away from a guy because of some stupid technicality, that's *weak,* and I've already appealed it. I'll tell you the thing that bothers me more than anything else, though, and that's that Brinkman was involved. I don't like to rip him, because I'm probably gonna get fined, but I am gonna rip him. We've been having problems with him all year, beginning in Kansas City with Wilson. This guy is *bustin'* us.

"I don't want any favors from the umpires, I don't want any *edge.* Let's just put Gossage against Brett and see what happens. Well, you saw what happened—four hundred and fifty feet away.

"I just can't *believe* this. But as soon as I saw Brinkman was going to be making the decision, as soon as they carried the bat out for him to look at, I said 'Oh, God. . . .' "

Martin, in the unaccustomed position of defending an umpire's judgment, was all sweet reason in the Yankee clubhouse. Nettles had noticed the extra pine tar on Brett's bat during the series the Yankees

< 88 >

had played in Kansas City just after the All-Star break, but the Yankees had said nothing at the time because "you don't call a guy on it if he makes an out, and this was really the first time Brett had hurt us." Asked if he thought the extra pine tar gave Brett any advantage, Martin said, "I don't know. You'd have to ask Brett that; he's the one uses it, so he probably thinks there is. All I know is there's a rule—it cost us a hit one time in Minnesota when Thurman was batting—and it says 'eighteen inches.' So I guess today, it was a *dis*advantage." He smiled, then concluded, "Sure turned out to be a lovely Sunday, didn't it?"

The Yankees might have been aware of the pine tar, but in their shock after Brett's hit they nearly blew their opportunity. Rick Cerone had been catching, and with Brett halfway around the bases he picked up the discarded bat. "I knew there was something I was supposed to check it for," he said, "but for a minute I couldn't even remember what. I thought it might have been loaded or something, but it felt all right, so I flipped it back down toward the batboy. Then I hear Nettles and Zimmer *screaming* from the dugout, and they're yelling, 'Pine tar, pine tar,' and all of a sudden I remembered. By then the batboy had the bat, though, so I yelled 'Hey,' and went running after him, 'Gimme that sucker.' "

"That was the big thing," said Zimmer. "If they get that bat back in the dugout, it's all over. They get it in the rack and there's no way you can tell what bat it was. Even if you can talk the umpires into looking at it, they could hand the umps a goddamn *cane* and there'd be no way to prove he hadn't used it."

Gossage, though he was by now sharing in the general sense of disbelieving elation, had at least initially been more preoccupied with the fact that the ball had been hit. "I knew about the bat, all right. I knew about it in Kansas City, 'cause Nettles had told me about it then. But all I could think was, 'Shit, he hit it out of here.' And I'll tell you, that sombitch is fucking *Houdini,* man. He can fucking hit. The man is amazing. They had that pitch at ninety-six on the speed gun, and it was up and in. Rick said if he hadn't hit it out, he would have chipped it into the net. He's a *great* hitter. I think next time I'm gonna go to the old LaRoche and give him a lob—or maybe roll it in."

Did he think it was in some sense unfair that Brett should lose the

< 89 >

home run. "Hell, no. A rule's a rule, and is he gonna be heartbroken if they find me out there with an itty-bitty piece of sandpaper tucked in my glove? You wanna know what I think? I think 'Tough shit.' "

On that note, the Yankees departed for Texas. They were on a roll, having won nine of their last ten games, including both the pine-tar victory and an extraordinary ninth-inning victory in which Steve Kemp, hustling as always, had scored all the way from first when a freak Yankee Stadium wind blew Don Baylor's routine pop foul out of the seats—where everyone in the park except Kemp believed it was certain to land—and about two inches inside the foul line. Feeling blessed by fate, umpires, and their own alert play, the team was more confident than it had been at any time since spring training. And confidence *matters*.

"Streaks for a team," said Roy Smalley, "are like streaks for a hitter. Most hitters are pretty streaky, and even though the mechanics of your swing might not change in any significant way no matter whether you're hot or cold, it's actually easier to hit the ball when you're riding a streak. When I'm goin' good—when I go up there knowing I'm gonna get a hit—I actually do see the ball better, and it's *easy* to hit. I can get a hit off anyone. At other times, and I swear you could look at the tapes all day and not see a difference in the swing, *you* could get me out.

"The mystery, I guess, is how you keep a streak going for as long as you can. It's got to end sometime, or it wouldn't be a streak, and maybe some of it is luck. I know that a lot of my streaks have ended when I've gone out and hit the ball hard four times in a row and come up empty, but they've stayed alive when I've been jammed and flared a couple of singles. Because streaks are so much mental—because your mechanics don't really seem to have all that much influence on 'em—you could argue that they are *result*-oriented, not process-oriented."

Perhaps, then, the great virtue of the pine-tar victory for the Yankees wasn't just the addition of a single number to their win column, but that the positive result—however oddly achieved—had kept their streak going. At a minimum, to have lost that game on Brett's home run (though if the game had been completed, the Yankees might well have pulled it out; Dan Quisenberry was unavailable for Kansas City,

< 90 >

and the remainder of their bullpen was surely hittable) would very likely have brought a sharp halt to the streak. "There are," said Cerone, "losses and *losses*. Even if you're really hot—like five out of six three times in a row is pretty hot, right?—you're gonna have some losses. Certain ones, though, you can just forget. You wake up in the morning and they're gone; it's like they never happened. But any time you lose with two outs in the ninth inning, that's a *bad* loss. That's one that'll stay with you for a while."

Certainly the Yankees played the Texas series as if they'd forgotten how to lose. They won the first game when, down a run in the ninth, Winfield went with the pitch and drove a two-run triple into the right-center gap; the second on Steve Balboni's grand slam, and the third on come-from-behind extra-base hits from Campaneris and Kemp. The twelve-out-of-thirteen streak moved them from fourth place into a tie for the division lead, the first time they'd been there since April 16, 1982.

They were, however, very much aware that the pine-tar victory could be taken away from them by the Kansas City protest. There was, it seemed, an ambiguity in the rules. While there was no doubt that Brett had hit his home run with an illegal bat, the provisions citing the penalty for using *that specific kind* of illegal bat appeared to be in conflict. On the one hand, it was clear that use of an illegal bat was an automatic out, but another section specified that illegal bats with too much pine tar on them were—perhaps merely—to be removed from the game. When the league ruled on Kansas City's protest, it wasn't going to be an automatic call.

Prior to each of the Texas games, Martin held what amounted to lawyers' discussions in his office. The participants weren't actually attorneys but the usual parade of scouts, old friends, and baseball writers, who pored over the rule books in a typically scholarly fashion. Everyone kept coming back to the same point—the rules were ambiguous—but Martin wouldn't take ambiguity for an answer.

Martin, of course, doesn't have much tolerance for ambiguity in any area of his life: writers are either allies or out to get him, players are either "true Yankees" or "horseshit," and Steinbrenner is either the greatest owner in the history of baseball or an ignorant meddler. The clear drawing of lines is inherent in the paranoid world view, but it's very much a part of baseball as well. When there's a close play

< 91 >

on the bases, the runner is either safe or out; the sign of "I dunno" is not in the umpires' repertoire. In at least that sense, baseball is markedly different from sports like basketball or football, where every event doesn't need to be judged. Often, for instance, one will see a collision of bodies on a basketball court that *must* be either a charge or a block—but there's no whistle, and it's as though the play had never existed. In Martin's game, that simply cannot happen; baseball has a judgment for everything.

The code underlying these judgments is contained in a relatively slim blue volume, *The Official Rules of Baseball*. Together with some supplementary instructions—for umpires, for scorers—these rules should cover just about every imaginable situation. Most baseball managers, Martin included, *know* the rules—not just in their minds but in their bloodstreams. For a good part of every year, they live by that blue book; teams have won games, and lost them, because a manager did, or did not, know his rules.

But Martin, even more than most managers, is a scholar of the rule book. Part of this is rooted in nothing more complicated than his desire to win; if he knows the rules better than the other manager, and perhaps even better than the umpires, his team may gain an edge. And on very rare occasions—Brett's bat providing an example—that edge may mean an extra number in the Yankees' 'W' column. Even beyond that, however, the rules are a comfort to him. In the whirling series of changes that have been his life, the rules are a constant. There are modifications from year to year, usually as a result of one manager or another finding a loophole and taking advantage of it, but these are for the most part clarifications of the rules-makers' intent rather than wholesale rewritings. Raised Catholic, and still a churchgoer, Martin believes in the *notion* of rules, and those that govern baseball give an order to his professional life. In a sense, Martin is an intuitive Hobbesian. If life turns out to be the war of each against all, he's prepared to fight. But projection is a powerful psychological force, and at least partly because he's all too familiar with fighting—and knows *how* he fights—he welcomes the baseball compacts.

Finally, like a lot of self-taught adults, Martin is slightly embarrassed by, and has an unjustified confidence in, the printed word. He brings to it none of the intellectual's confident skepticism, and even years of being slagged by various baseball writers haven't changed a

< 92 >

fundamental attitude not all that different from the one a junior high school kid brings to the encyclopedia. If it's in the book, it's true.

So when the rules of baseball appeared to contradict themselves, Martin felt more than disappointed or confused, he felt *betrayed*. Through the entire Texas series, he couldn't keep his mind off that betrayal. In the midst of conversations about some relatively important present Yankee concerns—for example, when Griffey's injured hamstring would heal so he could again play, and who would leave the roster to make room for him—Martin would veer off to recapitulate yet again the ambiguities of the pine-tar rules. Worrying at them as though they were a bit of corn stuck between his teeth, he spent hours trying to find a way in which they *had* to make him right.

But he couldn't. Neither, of course, could anybody find the phrase or sentence that would *have* to make him wrong. It wasn't for lack of trying, however—not only for Martin but also for the legions who argued over it in bars and newspaper columns all across the country. Finally, Martin was reduced to a quasi-political argument: "I don't honestly see any other thing they can do but honor the umpires. If the umpires make that kind of decision, after taking all the time they did to make up their minds, then the league has to stand by them. They stick up for everything else the umpires do, why should this be the exception?

"Of course," he continued, "if they do reverse the umps, I'd have the right to protest." Suddenly realizing the implications of what he'd just said, he importuned the reporters present, "Please don't print that right away, okay? I don't want Lee MacPhail reading that in the papers tomorrow, 'cause he'll think I'm trying to threaten him." Then, having already lost the decision and appealed it in his mind, he brightened again: "They *have* to honor the umps. If they don't, then they're saying that everything in the rule book doesn't mean anything. They gotta stick with the umps."

Outside the manager's office, the players were debating the decision as well. But most of them lacked Martin's patience, or perhaps his obsessiveness, and at one point in the debate Gossage finally said, "Hell, this whole thing is crazy. We oughta just be out there playin' baseball, and we're all sittin' around here like a bunch of fuckin' lawyers. Doesn't any fucking body remember that this is a *game* we're talkin' about, not some Supreme Court decision? There's too many

< 93 >

lawyers in baseball already. What we should do is settle it the same way we did when we were kids: Play a 'do-over.' Just pick the game up in the ninth, two outs and a runner on, with Brett coming up."

And if that's the way the league decided, what would he throw to Brett this time? "Nothing, man, not one fuckin' thing. I'd *walk* the cocksucker."

But he wasn't going to get the chance, for during the Yankees' off-day in Chicago, MacPhail announced his decision: The home run is good, and the Royals lead 5–4, with two out in the top of the ninth; the game to be completed as soon as possible, probably on the teams' next common off-day, August 18.

Martin had stayed an extra night in Texas in order to get some fishing in with his son, Billy Joe, who lived not far from the Rangers' Stadium, so he received the news in private, but as the word flashed from player to player in Chicago, the Yankees seemed stunned. Genuinely shocked by the decision, their nearly universal reaction was, "How can he *do* this to us?"

Well, it wasn't easy. The umpires had based their decision on two sections of the rule book. Rule 6.06*(a)* says that "a batter is out for illegal action when he hits an illegally batted ball." Under the definitions, a ball hit with an illegal bat is an illegal ball, and the "out" call is mandatory. Rule 1.10 deals with the legality of bats, and section *(a)* specifies that "the bat handle, for not more than 18 inches from the end, may be covered or treated with any material (including pine tar) to improve the grip . . ." and adds that no substance meant to improve the distance factor of the bat or to cause an unusual reaction on the baseball can be used even within the eighteen-inch limit. Such substances are specifically discussed in rule 6.06, which in section *(d)* specifies that, if such substances or alterations are found on a bat, "in addition to being called out, the player shall be ejected from the game and may be subject to additional penalties as determined by the League President."

Up to this point, the language seems unambiguous. If a batter hits the ball with an illegal bat, including one in which pine tar extends more than eighteen inches up the handle, he's out. If he hits it with a specific *sort* of illegal bat—one that is corked, grooved, nail-studded or, as Graig Nettles's once was, hollowed out and stuffed with high-

< 94 >

bounce rubber balls—he's not only out but out of the game, and may be suspended or fined as well. Since all hands agree that the pine tar extended some twenty-four inches up Brett's bat, the umpires had no choice but to call him out. This relatively straightforward interpretation is supported by American League Regulation 4.23 issued to umpires: "Official playing rule 6.06*d* prohibits the use of doctored bats. However the use of pine tar in itself shall not be considered doctoring the bat. The 18 inch rule will not be cause for ejection or suspension." The unmistakable implication of this language is that it *will,* however, be subject to an automatic "out" call under rule 6.06 *(a)*. It exempts that sort of bat from two of the three possible penalties, but lets the third stand.

If this were the sum total of major league rules and regulations covering pine-tar-treated bats, even a lawyer arguing Kansas City's side of the case would have had a tough time putting together a brief. But there is one other mention. A section of rule 1.10*(b)*—added *after* Munson had been called out in the 1975 game against the Twins—specifies that "material, including pine tar, which extends past the 18 inch limitation shall cause the bat to be removed from the game."

As written, this rule would seem to cover situations in which the umpires notice, or have called to their attention, an excess of pine tar *prior* to a ball being hit. In his decision, for instance, MacPhail noted that "it is probable that a batter attempting to use a bat clearly outside other general requirements of rule 1.10 (such as colored bats, etc.) would not be permitted to do so," adding that "the general procedure, when noticed by umpires or complained about by the opposing team, has been to require the use of a new bat or require that the old bat be cleaned up." Such a penalty *after* a ball has been hit is no penalty at all.

MacPhail never ruled on the Munson case; no protest was heard because the Yankees won the game. In September of that year, however, there was a protest involving pine tar which Kansas City also won. John Mayberry, then with the Royals, had hit two home runs in a game against the California Angels, and California protested on the grounds that he'd used excessive pine tar. Though this protest was filed prior to the language change about removing the bat from the game, MacPhail nonetheless rejected it. One key difference, as the fact of *two* hits makes clear, was that the California protest hadn't been

< 95 >

as timely as Martin's action; but in upholding the umpires' decision, MacPhail had written, "I would not consider that a ball hit with a bat with pine tar too far from the handle was necessarily an illegally batted ball under rule 6.06*(a),* as one hit with a bat not conforming to rule 1.10. Although rule 1.10 limits a foreign substance to 18 inches from the handle, we are not talking about a material that improves the reaction or distance factor of the bat."

In fact, MacPhail claimed in his 1983 decision that "the provision restricting the distance pine tar can extend up the barrel of the bat was primarily intended to keep from spoiling the ball and requiring new balls to be constantly brought into the game. Conversations with several members of the Rules Committee reinforce this belief." At least one member of that committee with whom MacPhail talked, George Sisler, found that claim overstated. "I wouldn't say that worry about replacing the ball, about slowing up the game, was *primary,*" he said. "It was *a* consideration, but the real difficulty wasn't so much the need to replace a spoiled ball as what happened to that ball while it was still in play. If the ball's got a big smudge on one side of it, it's going to be harder for fielders to read it—particularly if you get a chipped or spinning foul. Also," he added, "there was some concern that if pine tar went too far up the barrel, a player could bury nail heads under it, or that it might disguise the gluing on a corked bat. It's not the most important rule in the book, not even the most important rule about bats, but it's not just a technicality either."

MacPhail was not persuaded by such arguments, and for the first time in his ten years as league president overruled his umpires and upheld the Kansas City protest. "Although Manager Martin and his staff should be commended for their alertness," he wrote, "it is the strong conviction of the League that games should be won and lost on the playing field—not through technicalities of the rules—and that every reasonable effort consistent with the spirit of the rules should be made to so provide."

As Roy Smalley said at the time, "I wasn't aware there was one rule book for rules and one for spirit," but MacPhail's interpretation, though perhaps overly ingenious, was in no sense dishonorable. The spirit of the rules is important, and one reason baseball draws more fans than debate tournaments is that baseball games are won and lost on the field, not in the minds of judges. The league president, then,

< 96 >

was trying to preserve the *essence* of the game, but even by MacPhail's standard, there are problems with his decision.

The question raised by MacPhail's appeal to the spirit of the rules is whether Brett had inadvertently broken a relatively unimportant regulation or whether he had deliberately cheated. Saying there was no evidence that pine tar produced a livelier or more powerful bat (a claim the Yankees debated only half-heartedly and after the fact), MacPhail concluded the former.

In fact, however, Brett *was* cheating. Partly as an effort to speed the progress of their games, the American League Rules Committee had passed a series of new regulations during the off-season. One of these forbade batters to leave the batting box for additional pine tar once they had entered it. For most players, being unable to use the pine-tar rag during their turn at bat was a relatively minor inconvenience; most hitters now wear batting gloves, which, like pine tar, aid their ability to grip the bat. But Brett, as he'd said in the locker room, believed that he hit better without gloves (whether this is *actually* true or not is unknown and, to some degree, irrelevant, for it's clear that a hitter's confidence level does affect his performance), and he was therefore unusually dependent on gripping agents like pine tar. The reason he had pine tar beyond the eighteen-inch limit—well beyond the point where he gripped the bat—was essentially for storage purposes. Routinely, between pitches, he reached up the bat handle to grab some of the extra gripping agent he'd warehoused there. In sneaking around the new rule, however, he broke the one on which Martin and the Yankees had called him. And he broke it not out of ignorance—both he and Howser admitted that various umpiring crews had made him clean his bat off "three or four times" during the year—but deliberately and recurringly. Even by MacPhail's generous "spirit of the rules" standard, his decision to overrule the umpire seems to have been misguided. However tainted the Yankees' victory might have been, it shouldn't have been taken away from them.

But it was, and that was that. Though he'd earlier talked about the possibility of an appeal, Martin knew that the gesture would be futile; appeals, like the original protest, are decided by the league president. Instead, he focused on some practical questions about the conditions under which the remainder of the pine-tar game would be played.

< 97 >

"What about Quisenberry? Are they gonna be able to bring him in and pitch the ninth inning against us? That wouldn't be right, because he couldn't have pitched the ninth that day. He'd gone five and two-thirds the day before."

He was also concerned about when it might be played. No more games were scheduled between the two teams, and at his press conference MacPhail had suggested that August 18—an open day for both —was a possible date. Martin didn't like this idea at all: "That's their day off, and in the middle of the pennant race they're gonna need those days. I wouldn't ask 'em to play on their day off—especially not to make up a game that shouldn't be played in the first place. It's probably gonna be up to them," he said, referring to the union contract that guarantees players a day off at least once every twenty days. "But I know if I was a player, *I'd* vote against it."

Though Martin had accepted the ruling as a *fait accompli,* he remained agitated by it. When Lee Walls came into the manager's office and asked, "Got the lineup, Skip?" Martin snapped, "I *never* make out the lineup 'til I find out who's healthy. Why don't you check with the trainer?"

On a higher pitch now, he returned to MacPhail's decision. "I had a feeling, a funny feeling. . . . But it still seems crazy to me. He's telling every kid in the country, 'Go ahead and cheat, use a dirty bat if you can get away with it. And even if you get caught, we won't do nothin' to you.' What's the sense of havin' a rule if they don't punish you for breakin' it? I'll tell you, when I kicked dirt on the umpires earlier— which was wrong—they didn't hesitate to suspend me. Why do the rules only count when *we* break 'em?

"I can hardly wait until one of our guys wants to go to the pine-tar rag and the umpire says no. I'll be right out there, 'Show me the rule! Show me the penalty!'"

In general, the players seemed more stunned—or maybe mystified —than angry. As Gossage put it, "A rule is a rule. If they're not gonna enforce it, why have it in the rule book?"

The question was one shared by almost every player in the locker room, and their unhappiness was only exacerbated by their helplessness. MacPhail's decision was to all intents and purposes final, and they didn't have the power to do anything about it. Apparently out of this frustration, Piniella suggested that "if the game does matter—

< 98 >

if the season ends up tied, or one of us is up by less than a game—baseball's gonna be in a bad predicament. It's gonna be more than a public relations problem, too. There's gonna be lawsuits. I know that if they try to take fifty thousand dollars out of my pocket, I'll sue the goddamn league."

Characteristically, Piniella came around to all the reporters within a few moments of making his threat, urging them not to print it. "I might do it anyway," he said, "but I don't want anybody reading about it and getting madder at us than they already are." Less characteristically, and perhaps as a result of their feeling so powerless (though maybe just because a forty-six-minute rain delay threw them off), the Yankees played flat, spiritless ball in the first Chicago game, getting only five hits off journeyman Jerry Koosman and losing 7–2. The only time all night they showed much energy was on the ride back to the hotel, when they second-guessed the bus driver's detours so vigorously and obscenely that at one point he jerked to a halt in the middle of the road and announced that he wasn't driving anybody anywhere until they shut up. Like a pack of cowed kids on a school outing, they did.

The next night was, if possible, even worse than the first. After taking an early 1–0 lead, they were unable to score, once taking themselves out of a one-out, runners-on-second-and-third situation with two strikeouts in a row. They lost 6–1, hitting into three double plays en route, and by the end of the game they were playing as though they'd given up. In the Chicago eighth, Julio Cruz sliced a sinking line drive to left center that fell just beyond Jerry Mumphrey's diving attempt; it rolled all the way to the wall for a triple because Winfield had nonchalanted his backup.

Perhaps in an effort to wake his team up—or perhaps to let off some of his own excess energies—Martin spent much of the night popping out of the dugout to bitch at the umpires. And when he wasn't actually out on the field, he was yelling at them from the bench, twice drawing admonitory visits from the plate umpire. The period of comparatively good behavior that had coincided with the Yankees' long hot streak was over.

For Martin, at least, the next day represented a further slide. He arrived at the park fresh from seeing George Brett interviewed on national television—"fuckin' foolin' around, *laughing*"—and he was

< 99 >

already angry. "Why wasn't there somebody on television telling them that Lee MacPhail made the worst decision in the history of baseball? You won't see that, 'cause there'd be nobody laughin' about it. It's too serious.

"Should I be a television comedian now, and just go out and break every rule in the book? Not pay any attention to the rules at all? When the pitcher goes to his mouth and they call a balk, I'll come runnin' out and say it's a *technicality*? That's no way to play baseball—and it's no way for kids to learn to play baseball either. Kids gotta learn to play by the rules."

Though this concern for the youth of America comes somewhat oddly from a man who demonstrated that kicking dirt at an umpire was acceptable behavior, it was very likely sincere. But Martin was actually less worried about what MacPhail's decision might do to impressionable kids than what it had already done to the Yankees. "I'm gonna have a little meeting right after batting practice," he said. "I think this thing has started to affect them. They're dead right now, not running the bases well, not swingin' their bats at all."

But shouldn't a team of professionals be able to rise above that on their own? "Listen, I think it's a human thing in this situation to get down a little bit. It's like when your brother did something wrong and you got your ass whipped for it. When you feel you've been wrongly hurt, you sulk. You're pissed at your parents, you go into your room and sulk, and you—all on your own—miss some kind of fun that's going on outside. It's a gut feeling, and while you can say that the guys ought to be able to get over it on their own—they *aren't* little kids —one thing I've learned as a manager is, 'Never take anything for granted.' *You* know they know, but don't take it for granted. Don't take nothing for granted."

Whatever he said, the Yankees looked like a different team. On this afternoon, their mistakes came from playing aggressively, not lazily. Though the result on the bases was similar to the previous day's when Winfield turned Rudy Law's first-inning single into a triple by trying to make an impossible diving catch on it, Winfield's attitude was visibly different. It was no surprise when, after a hardscrabble game in which the Yankees led twice, trailed twice, and were tied in the eighth, they piled up six runs in the eleventh—including a Baylor grand slam—and put away a 12–6 victory.

< 100 >

Martin, however, was not around to watch the results. He, along with Rick Cerone, had been booted in the fifth inning by plate umpire Dale Ford (who had a busy day, also tossing Chicago's manager, Tony LaRussa, in the eleventh). Martin's usual postgame press conference was delayed by a meeting with general manager Murray Cook, who wanted to caution him not to say anything that might get him into further trouble. Martin had been all over the umpires all day, and Cook wanted him to cool it.

Cook wasn't the only one worried that Martin might have been a little too rough on the umpires. Though the Yankees got the call that counted when Robertson slid home with the tie-breaking run in the eleventh (this was the play over which LaRussa got himself chucked), every other close play in the game had gone Chicago's way, and Don Baylor was concerned: "Today reminded me a lot of the first part of the season. It's like there was a *tendency* on the part of the umpires —I don't know if it's against Billy or what—for plays to go the other way. For a while there, it had kind of mellowed out, but Billy's been a lot more active the last few days, and here it is back again. Six or seven close plays today, and every one but the last went against us.

"I used to see the same thing happen in Baltimore a lot when Earl was managing there. I don't know if it's a fraternity thing, but the umpires all kind of stick together; if you get down on one of them, the others are gonna back him up. I know I'd hate to look back at the end of a year and see where a close call one way or another would have made a difference in whether we won the division.

"I'm not saying that Billy's always wrong, or anything. I know once after he got thrown out in Texas and we came back to New York, I was standing right next to him and one umpire's swearing at him, *really* swearing at him. Billy says something back, and he's gone. That was wrong, but maybe that umpire wouldn't have been swearing at him if he hadn't gone through the dirt-kicking thing in Texas. It looked to me like the umpire was trying to intimidate him. Thing is, the man isn't going to be intimidated, so they all keep fighting each other, and pretty soon you start wondering why it is that home plate has all of a sudden gone from seventeen inches to twenty-two when we're batting."

Martin, when his door finally opened, surely didn't seem intimidated. Neither, however, did he start out particularly intimidat-

< 101 >

ing; perhaps as a result of Cook's visit—and certainly as a result of the win—he was low-keyed and laughing when he began to explain why he'd been chucked. "To begin with," he said, "I went out there to complain about Cerone being thrown out. The umpire said he thought Rick had pushed him, and I tried to explain that he'd tripped and *fallen* into him." The game films bore out Martin's contention. Cerone, whirling to protest a "safe" call on a sliding Chicago runner, had caught his spikes on the plate and fallen to his knees. In order to keep himself from pitching over completely, he'd grabbed at Ford's knees. Ford, who had pointedly turned his back on the plate purposely to *avoid* an argument, instantly gave the ejection sign, which is automatic for bumping. Martin went around to the other umpires, hoping they would confirm his account, but they all claimed they were looking elsewhere. "I don't understand it," said Martin, unknowingly offering support for Baylor's theory, "Everybody's watching some other play, and the only play there *was* was at home."

"But that wasn't why I got thrown out," he continued. "I got Butch out there for Cerone, and after only five throws, Ford is telling him he's gotta start playing. I know sure as hell when I was a player, five throws couldn't get *my* arm ready. I don't want to risk an injury to Butch, especially when he's my last catcher, so I just went over to Ford and said, 'You don't know the rules, pal.' Because there's nothin' at all in there says someone coming in for an ejected catcher is limited to five throws.

"Of course that don't matter to him. I bet a hundred dollars that sombitch can't even read. He thinks manual labor's a Mexican, the dumb cocksucker." Despite his having just called Ford a cocksucker, Martin's anger was at this point largely theatrical, a conscious—if elephantine—performance. "Let me quote you the rule," he said, brandishing his battered copy of the rule book. "There's nothing at all in here says he's gotta stop Butch after five throws. And I ought to know, I been sittin' in here readin' this sombitch for the last three innings. But with this crew out there on the field, you know what this rule book is good for? Good for deer hunting, and that's all. Next time you go deer hunting, make sure you got a copy with you, 'cause you never know when you're gonna need toilet paper. The league president *doesn't* follow it, and these dumb bastards *can't.*"

< 102 >

Merely thinking about MacPhail—or perhaps merely articulating the name that had consistently been in the back of his thoughts— seemed to cause Martin to shift gears. With intensity and volume rising, he went on, "For three weeks now, you haven't seen me on the field hardly. How come one crew comes in here and every day since Lee's decision I've had to be out there a half-dozen times. Is it just that this crew is having a bad series, or is there something about the decision? I was honest-to-God worried today, I'll tell you. I don't mean to say there's any conspiracy or anything like that, but *every* decision went against us."

Asked about Baylor's theory, which certainly seemed to fit with what he'd just been saying, Martin responded, "I don't know if it's me or not. Earl was always on the umpires with Baltimore, and they won their pennants. Hell, *I've* always been on the umpires whenever they've screwed up, and I don't think I've ever been through a series like this one.

"I think it's that they know of the ruling by Lee MacPhail against us, and they feel they've got a little freer rein now. It's like there's a little backlash out there. And the thing is," he continued, "if that's what's goin' on, who's gonna call 'em on it?

"You know what I'd like to see in the papers? Just once, I'd like to read about the league president saying an umpire was wrong. Not that he's fined, not that he is fired, but 'He did the wrong thing.' " This was, of course, precisely what he had been reading ever since Mac-Phail overruled the umpires in the pine-tar decision, but Martin was heating up at this point, and no one pointed out his unintended irony. "But they can do whatever they want to and get away with it. This series here, I'm gettin' *tired* from walking out there so much. That can't be an accident; there's gotta be some reason for it.

"And maybe it's not Lee. Maybe it's me. From what you say, some of the players are thinking the umpires are taking it out on Billy and that's hurting the ball club. Well, the players have as good a look at what's going on out there as you can get, and if they're thinking that, maybe I should step down as manager. If I lost this game today, I was honestly thinking about that while I was sittin' here. But," he brightened, "we didn't lose, and the guy in the other dugout got tossed too, so maybe it *is* just an accident, a coincidence. I sure hope so."

< 103 >

"Anyway," he added, concluding a process in which he'd gradually led himself deeper and deeper into a conspiracy theory before perhaps finding his way out, "the guys really showed me something today. Everything was goin' against them, but they kept battling. I think they may have the pine tar out of their systems by now. We're gonna win here tomorrow, then go up to Toronto and kick ass."

But Martin's upswing turned out to be brief and fragile, for a reporter who had been down in the umpires' dressing room came in with Ford's version of what had happened on the field. Ford said he'd talked to Wynegar, and that he'd given the signal to play ball only after Wynegar had said he was ready. According to Ford, Martin's getting all over him on the field had been nothing but harrassment.

Martin leapt to his feet, charging over to the reporter as though he were charging the umpire, and began screaming. "Liar!" he shouted, his voice echoing around the tiny office. "Liar! He never fuckin' talked to Butch. *I* talked to Butch." Martin, his face empurpled, had moved within inches of the reporter and was spraying saliva with every furious phrase. "He's a stone liar, a stone fucking liar, and you can ask Butch."

Among all the possible Yankees, Martin couldn't have named a more reliable witness. Pick your phrase—straight arrow, boy scout, *integer vitae scelerisque purus*—Wynegar was it. In covering a team day after day, season after season, reporters get to know the players pretty well, and it was without exception Wynegar to whom they turned when they were seeking the facts behind some particular dispute. He might occasionally say he didn't know, or more rarely that whatever had happened really wasn't his business so he didn't want to talk about it; but when he did talk, his version had always proven reliable. He was by no means the most interesting player to talk to about nonbaseball matters, and certainly not the most creative player on the field, but even when the truth was embarrassing to him, he always delivered it. From time to time, almost every other player on the club had dissembled, and of course Martin and Steinbrenner were both practiced liars, but Wynegar didn't seem to know *how* to lie. If he confirmed Martin's version of what had happened on the field, Ford was indeed "a stone liar." And this time, Wynegar unhesitatingly supported Martin. No, he said, Ford hadn't said a word to him, hadn't even made a gesture, before giving the signal to start play.

< 104 >

Still, accurate as his comment about Ford had apparently been, Martin had surely gone further than he'd intended to—and certainly well beyond the position he and Murray Cook had staked out. It was neither the first time nor the last such a thing would happen—it often seemed that as soon as Martin let *any* of his anger spill, *all* of it came spewing out—and despite the inevitable newspaper stories about his outburst that appeared the following morning, Martin seemed unworried as he prepared for the next day's game. Although he'd been warned at the time of his last suspension that any further attacks on the umpires' integrity would be a cause for disciplinary action, Martin pointedly refused to express any regret for what he'd said, and anticipated no problems with the league president. "I don't expect to be hearing from Lee MacPhail," he said, "because I didn't cuss the guys out or anything. I just said Dale Ford didn't tell the truth, that's all."

This rosy prediction turned out to be wrong; Richie Phillips, head of the umpires union, had already called for MacPhail to suspend Martin, and Martin was to draw a two-day suspension. He'd also been wrong in his prediction a day earlier: the Yankees had not recaptured the habit of winning. In the first inning of that night's game, Ray Fontenot gave up his first major league home run. It was a genuine monster, too. The massive Greg Luzinski got all the way around on a 2–2 pitch and hit it *over* the left-field stands—only the twenty-second time in history that a ball had gone on or over the roof. As if this weren't enough, an SRO crowd of 44,812 White Sox fans rose and bid farewell to the ball with a chorus of their home run anthem "Hey, Hey, Na-Na, Good-Bye." And fireworks boomed from beyond the center-field wall. And the pinwheel lights atop the scoreboard twirled giddily. There is probably no good place for a rookie pitcher to yield his first homer, but a packed Comiskey Park must be the worst.

Fontenot got another chance to witness the whole display in the third inning, when Luzinski's only slightly more modest drive carried into the upper deck in left. Songs, lights, fireworks, and a 4–0 Chicago lead. The Yankees were held to six hits, and averted a shutout only because one of them was a Winfield home run. The Yankee road trip, which had started out so well, was now at 4–3, and in the next night's doubleheader against Toronto the Yankees were going with their two weakest starters, Keough and Shirley.

< 105 >

For the first time in the Toronto Blue Jays' brief history, the All-Star break had come and gone without seeing them sink inexorably toward the bottom of the standings. Buoyed by a fine young pitching staff, they had matured into pennant contenders, a development their long-suffering fans had greeted first with polite skepticism and then with unrestrained joy. For the twi-night doubleheader that opened the series against their historic tormentors, an all-time-record crowd of 45,102 packed into Exhibition Stadium. The stadium had originally been designed for Canadian football, with its twenty-five-yard end zones and hundred-and-ten-yard field, and the baseball diamond, with a temporary right-field fence stretched across the field at about the fifty-yard line, was jammed into a corner of the sprawling Astroturf playground. The stands, however, remained unadapted, for a while abutting the left-field wall, but finally abandoning it as it gently began its curve. Late arrivals for the series' opener wound up sitting at the far end zone, about 800 feet from home plate. They didn't seem to mind, however, and stayed well on into the night, cheering and singing as the Blue Jays swept both games.

The first game, even from 800 feet away, was probably worth the price of admission, especially for Blue Jay fans. The Yankees hit five home runs, held leads of 6–2, 6–3, 6–5, 8–7, and 9–8 before managing to lose 10–9 in the tenth inning. Though they obviously seemed to have gotten their bats back, the Yankees, playing on the unfamiliar artificial turf, were almost unimaginably awful in the field. The Blue Jays scored two unearned runs in the fifth, when an easy double-play ball caught a seam and skipped past Roy Smalley, and even more dramatically tied the game off Gossage in the ninth when Nettles just managed to stab another routine double-play grounder that found a seam but couldn't get the ball out of his glove's webbing in time to make a play. In the second game, despite three more Yankee home runs (making a total of eight that the pinstripes managed to send down the toilet), the Blue Jays waltzed home, 13–6. The Yankees might have been a championship club on paper, but on the field they looked like the Bad News Bears.

There were excuses to be made for the Yankees—especially for the way they somnambulated through the second game after having arrived in Toronto at 4:30 in the morning—but it's also true that they didn't play like contenders. Winning teams don't give away games in

< 106 >

August, and the Yankees played as though they had only half a mind on the game—with the rest, presumably, formulating appeals to Lee MacPhail's pine-tar ruling.

Martin, at any rate, seemed finally to have gotten past the pine-tar game. Before the doubleheader, when some Toronto reporters came into his office for the ritual pregame chat, he responded for the first time to a question about the MacPhail ruling with a courteous, but firm, "I think that's been talked about enough." That does not mean, however, that the manager was fully concentrating on the upcoming games. He'd finally learned about Phillips's request that he be suspended, and was beginning to be worried that he might indeed have gone too far in Chicago. Typically, his defense turned into an attack. "I don't understand it," he said. "Every time I do *anything,* Richie Phillips is asking for me to be suspended. But this is just stupid. Ford told the press that he'd talked to Butch Wynegar, and I said that wasn't the truth. And for that—which *was* the truth—Richie Phillips wants Lee to suspend me. I'd like to see Phillips fall off a bridge.

"He says it's because I'm some kind of 'repeat offender,' but what about Tony LaRussa? He's been thrown out four times this year, and I've only been tossed out three. But you don't see anybody calling for *him* to be suspended.

"This makes a lot of sense, right? It's really good for the game of baseball to suspend the manager. How many people do you think come to the ballpark to see Richie Phillips? Richie Phillips better stick to his lawyer's business and pay his bills in Philadelphia—which," he added in a gratuitous and unprovable smear, "I hear he owes a lot of."

By the next night, Martin's concern about his possible suspension had given way to concern about his bullpen. Not only had all the relievers he'd used been woefully inadequate during the opening doubleheader, he'd used all that he had, and there were no arms left in the bullpen. Guidry was starting and was, under normal circumstances, a good bet to throw a complete game, but at least partly to save his bullpen for this series, Martin had let Guidry throw a complete, 152-pitch game in Chicago, and the little left-hander might well have been tired.

Still, Martin's lack of worry seemed genuine, not whistling in the dark, when he said, "If Guidry'd been tired after Chicago, I'd be

< 107 >

concerned, but he wasn't tired at all. He didn't have his good stuff in that game the other night, so he threw a lot of curves and changes, and that could even make him stronger.

"Besides," Martin continued, "a pitcher's chemical makeup is a little different every time he pitches. I keep count of the throws only so's I know when a pitcher *might* be running out of gas. With that and the speed gun, you know." Guidry, whose delivery is so mechanically perfect that Sammy Ellis believes "he could throw forever and not hurt his arm," did provide the desperately needed complete game, but he was a long way from overpowering; he gave up thirteen hits as the Blue Jays made it three in a row, 6–2.

For the second straight night, the Yankee clubhouse was funereal. This was, it seemed, more than the usual postdefeat disappointment; the Yankees were beginning to doubt themselves. "We ran into three well-pitched games in Chicago," said Roy Smalley, "and you sort of say, 'Well, that's the way it sometimes is.' But we should have won that first game last night, and then—maybe because we'd screwed up the first—we just got blown out in the second. It's a real cause for concern, because now's the wrong time to be losing. And it's not like we're losing any one way, either—not something where you can say there's a definite weakness here and we better go to Columbus or a trade to fill it. One night we can't hit, one night we can't pitch, one night we can't field. But maybe the fact that it's *not* any one thing—that there's no fundamental problem you can point to—kind of suggests that we're just in one of those bad streaks that every team gets into a couple of times during the year. I sure hope so."

Though it might indeed have been no more than a bad streak, there were limits on how long the Yankees could stay mired in it without falling out of the pennant race. Martin had been doing a lot more juggling with his lineup than he had during the Yankees' recent hot spell; but beyond trying to shake the pieces around until he came up with a winning combination, there wasn't all that much he could do, and before the series' final game he was once again preoccupied with the Ford incident. In his office, he took a phone call from his friend and lawyer Eddie Sapir, then passed the phone over to a reporter so that Sapir could dictate a story that had appeared in Ford's hometown paper, the *Johnson City Press-Chronicle,* in June of 1981. Headlined "Ford Says Martin Is Vicious," the piece quoted the umpire as saying,

< 108 >

"I can tolerate Earl Weaver, the Orioles' manager, he's more like a clown. But Billy Martin is vicious. He'll hit you when your back is turned. I've never turned from a confrontation. I told him last year that he's a snake in the grass, and that's the type of person he is."

Whatever the accuracy of Ford's statement, one sentence stands out like a beacon of truth: "I've never turned from a confrontation." Perhaps it was left over from playing baseball as a kid and having had —whenever we had any—grownups as umpires, but I'd always tended to imagine that major league umpires were also, in relation to major league players, grownups: solemn, judgelike umpires upheld the rules while aggressive, naughty players tried to break them.

But that's not the way it is. Umpires and players are really a lot like each other, in age and in temperament. There are scrappy battlers and aloof superstars in both groups, and through long familiarity each has a pretty good line on the other. When you ask a dozen or so American League players to name the "best" or "fairest" umpires, a very small handful of names—Steve Palermo's most consistently—comes up with any regularity. And when you ask the same players to name outstanding red-asses among the umps, Dale Ford's name is almost always among them.

Yet I think my initial misconception—that umpires are faceless, passionless arbiters—is broadly shared by the general public, and Martin was delighted at the opportunity Ford had given him to prove it wasn't so. "How can this guy call my games fairly if he thinks I'm a vicious snake in the grass?" he asked. "No wonder I was all over the field in Chicago. I know there are umpires that don't like me. There are umpires that I don't like—hell, there are *people* I don't like —but the good umpires get by that. The guy I kicked dirt on down in Texas, I apologized to him, and he's been great to us. But Ford can't put his feelings behind him.

"I mean, what's he doing writing an article like that. That was in the middle of the goddamn baseball strike, and he's sitting at home mouthing off about me to some reporter. I'm here in my office, answering questions from the press, which is my *job,* and I point out that he's told an untruth. How come I'm the one gonna get suspended?

"And," he said, combining the pine-tar game with his pervasive sense of injustice, "what about George Brett? I don't want anything to happen to Brett, but when he came running out of the dugout like

< 109 >

that, he did bump three umpires. I'm glad Billy Martin didn't do that. Shit, I'd be down right now in Palm Springs playing golf with Leo Durocher."

The odds were still good that Martin would get a chance to work on his golf game. Ford apparently had, to use the Nixonian euphemism, "misspoken himself" in Chicago, and he'd certainly shot his mouth off during the strike, but Martin had been under strict instructions from the league not to challenge the integrity of the umpires. When you call someone a liar, that surely counts as such a challenge.

But at the end of the game—a nicely pitched duel in which the Yankees were outhit seven to six but which they won 3–1 for Rawley —Martin had something else to worry about. Dave Winfield was under arrest and had been charged with cruelty to animals. Just before the start of the Toronto fifth, he'd killed a seagull with a thrown ball. In a season which had included both the sublime (Righetti's no-hitter) and the ambiguous (the pine-tar game), we had finally come to the ridiculous.

That, at least, was how the players viewed the charge, and anyone even slightly familiar with the raucous, scavenging behavior of seagulls would be hard put to argue that they were wrong. That did not, however, affect the law. Precisely why the seagull should be specially protected under the Ontario provincial code is mysterious, but it is, and Winfield had certainly bagged one.

The Jays' stadium is near the Toronto waterfront, an easy commute for gulls, who regard baseball—with its attendant hot dog scraps and spilled popcorn—as a boon. As a rule, the hundreds of birds that cruise the stadium stay pretty much beyond the outfield fence, rising in a cloud when a large crowd roars and waiting for the game to end before they turn the seats into a cafeteria. Occasionally, a few birds will settle on the playing field itself, but they rarely stay for long. Between halves of the fifth inning, however, one appeared to be setting up permanent headquarters in short left center. Winfield, afraid that it would fly up in the middle of a play and distract him, told teammates on the bench that he flipped his final warmup toss toward the bird in order to scare it away. But the bird might have been short-hopped, and instead of flying away it sat and let the ball hit it. After a few minutes, as it gradually became obvious that this particular gull wasn't ever going to fly again, a ball boy came and carried it away.

< 110 >

By then, fans in the Toronto outfield had started to throw things at Winfield (who had, not incidentally, driven in two of the Yankees' three runs), and an officer of the Metropolitan Toronto Police who was attending the game had decided that Winfield had violated section 402 of the provincial code.

Winfield, notified on his way back to the clubhouse that he should dress promptly in order to accompany the arresting officer to a nearby station house, entered the locker room with his hands up. Amid the laughter and amazement, Martin was telling reporters that if the police "are gonna say he was that deliberate, they better look at some of the fucking throws he's made this year. This is the first time he's hit the cut-off man all season." And as Oscar Gamble danced around him yelling, "Get the handcuffs, get the handcuffs," Winfield was solemnly offering the press a somewhat revised version of what had happened: "The fans were on my case out there," he said, "because they thought I hit the bird deliberately. But it was unfortunate, not intentional. I didn't even see it there, and I was just tossing the ball back into the bullpen at the end of the warmups and it bounced into the bird." With that, he began to get dressed for his trip to the 14th Division of the Metropolitan Police.

Most of the Yankees treated this event as a sort of entertaining diversion—Nettles remarked that "the birds have been beating up on us all series; it's only fair that we get one back"—but the hunters among the Yankees—Gossage, Keough, and Guidry—were genuinely mystified. Gossage said, "You know, they must really hate us up here. I've killed *hundreds* of birds in Colorado and nothing's ever happened." Only Rudy May, who quietly removed a handful of hundred-dollar bills from his wallet and offered them to Winfield, had an immediate, practical reaction, and even he was unable to resist a quick jab of the needle—"Hey, Big Blood. You got your bail money pinned to your lapel?"—as Winfield and an embarrassed squad of Blue Jay officials went to join the arresting officer.

After that, the fun was over. The immediate practical effect of Winfield's arrest was to delay the flight home. For a couple of extra hours, the Yankees sat at a desolate airfield fifty miles outside Toronto, as they had missed the Metropolitan Airport's curfew. At the police station, Winfield was joined not only by the Blue Jay officials and the Yankees' traveling secretary, but by a representative

< 111 >

of the prosecutor's office and two staff members of the Humane Society; "A lot of people, actually—for a bird," said a Toronto police sergeant. And indeed it turned out to be. Though Winfield was formally charged and had to post $500 bond, senior officials from the prosecutor's office dropped the case as unprovable as soon as they reviewed it the following day.

Silly and wasteful as the whole event was—and nothing about it was any sillier than a two-page Steinbrenner statement demanding an apology from Toronto authorities and claiming that "I personally and I am sure our players as well care about wildlife in our country just as much as the Canadians do in their country"—it snapped the pine-tar spell. The Yankees even shrugged off the effects of Martin's unsurprising suspension, which was announced the day they returned home, and during the course of an undistracted week played solid baseball, taking two out of three from Detroit and three of four from Toronto. But by the time they reached Detroit on August 11, the pine-tar furor had begun all over again.

A couple of days earlier, in New York, MacPhail had announced that the remainder of the pine-tar game would indeed be scheduled for August 18. Steinbrenner, in a meeting with reporters, blasted the decision, saying that it would mean thirty-one days without a break for his players and that they "not only need a day off, they deserve one. . . . I'd rather forfeit than play the game," he continued, "but I don't know if that is fair to the players. If I had my way, I'd tell him to stick it in his ear, along with the decision." (This is, you will remember, the same George Steinbrenner who earlier threatened to fire Martin because he *didn't* take a day off away from the players by scheduling a mandatory punitive workout.)

Spurred by their bodies as well as by their owner, the players were of one mind about the game. They wanted it scheduled at the end of the season, to be played only if necessary. Believing that the basic agreement between the players union and the leagues specified a scheduled off day after no more than twenty games in a row, they voted to advise the league of their decision not to play the tentatively scheduled make-up game. This was only an advisory vote, just as the game was only tentatively scheduled, and when player rep Dave Winfield was asked what the team would do if MacPhail *ordered* them

< 112 >

to play, he hedged: "I'm sure everybody has an opinion on that. But the media, as you know, can influence negotiations, and you're not going to influence this one. You'll just have to come back tomorrow for the continuing soap opera."

When the Yankees reached Detroit, they learned not only that MacPhail had scheduled the game for August 18 but that he'd set a 6 P.M. start, confounding Steinbrenner's announced intention to put together an afternoon game and musical performance "for the kids and campers who'll be able to take advantage of specially reduced prices and be present at an historic occasion." Steinbrenner was furious, and in a conference call to Detroit told reporters that "I stand 100 percent behind Billy and the players on this. If they vote not to play, I'll back them. If it means forfeiting, if it means we lose the pennant, that's all right with me." Winfield, who'd not had a chance to meet with his fellow players, merely said, "This'll be interesting. Stay abreast." And Martin, for once calmer about something than either the players or the owner, preferred to hope for divine intervention. "Maybe," he said, "it'll rain."

Even Martin, however, was more distracted than he admitted. The Yankees had won the series opener on a tenth-inning Winfield home run, but despite two more Winfield homers and a deep double, lost the second in ten innings. In the eighth inning of that game, the Yankees broke a 5–5 tie when Willie Randolph reached second on a two-base error, Nettles walked, and Winfield hit an r.b.i. double so hard off the center-field wall that it bounced back too quickly for Nettles to score. With runners on second and third and one out, Griffey was the batter. On the first pitch, with Nettles racing home, Griffey attempted to put down a squeeze bunt, but missed. Given Nettles's speed, the squeeze attempt was suicidal indeed, and Griffey's deep fly to right on the next pitch was the third out instead of an r.b.i. sacrifice. With first base open, two runners in scoring position, and Baylor due at the plate next, Martin's call for the squeeze seemed unorthodox at best, but he dismissed questions about it after the game with an uncharacteristic "I have no comments." Later that night, he revealed that the team had installed new signs for this series and that he'd momentarily forgotten them. When he had casually leaned back against the dugout pole as Griffey came to the plate, he'd put the squeeze on, very likely costing the Yankees the game.

< 113 >

Despite taking that bad loss, the Yankees fared reasonably well on the short road trip, and came home with a respectable split. At the Stadium, however, the raree-show was going full blast. There were more player meetings, inflammatory Steinbrenner statements, and a complicated series of court actions. Operating, Steinbrenner insisted, without any prompting from the Yankees, some fans who'd held tickets to the original pine-tar game filed suit in New York State Supreme Court claiming they had a contractual right to be admitted to its completion. They requested that the game be enjoined until the court had time to hear their arguments, and the Yankees, not surprisingly, didn't oppose them. Believing that this theoretically adversary procedure was actually collusive, attorneys for the American League entered the case, and opposed the injunction.

But on the morning of the 18th, it was granted. The league immediately filed for an appeal, and a parade of lawyers and journalists headed south from the Bronx County Courthouse to the Appellate Division in lower Manhattan. There, despite dire warnings from Yankee attorney Roy Cohn of a riot, "a situation worse than Diana Ross," the injunction was lifted. The Yankees, announcing that they would admit holders of ticket stubs as well as purchasers of new tickets, didn't appeal, and the "historic event" finally took place.

The Yankees hadn't wanted to play it at all, of course, but they arrived at the stadium even flatter than one might have expected. Most of them had been following the day's courtroom drama over the radio, and as they'd tuned in they'd learned that Andre Robertson had been injured in an early-morning car crash on the West Side Highway. As he was driving a visiting friend back to her hotel at about five o'clock that morning, he'd turned his car over, and both he and his passenger had been taken to the hospital, where they remained on the critical list.

Given the unquestionable sadness that permeated the locker room before the game—and given as well the continuing circus that had led up to it—the pine-tar finale was mercifully brief. Also, at least partly because the Yankees had chosen not to promote it, virtually private. However, in the twelve minutes it took for the Royals to dispatch the Yankees, the handful in attendance did get to see one historic first.

Though the two teams were obviously the same that had faced each

< 114 >

other during the first eight and two-thirds innings, the original umpiring crew had been assigned elsewhere. Martin, thinking that this new crew of umpires—who had of course not seen the original game—*couldn't* rule on any appeal play, had pitcher George Frazier toss the ball in sequence to each of the three bases. When the umpires gave the "safe" signal, indicating that the Kansas City runners had indeed touched each base as they jogged around, Martin bounced onto the field—where he was greeted with signed affidavits from the original umpiring crew saying that the bases had been touched.

Despite the extremely anticlimactic nature of the event, it seemed to have drawn nearly every reporter in the western hemisphere, and *all* of them were in the Yankee clubhouse after the game. Most of the players, however, were hiding in either the players' lounge or the trainer's room—both off limits—until the crush eased. Roy Smalley was waylaid en route, however, and this normally most cooperative of interviewees certainly spoke for his absent teammates when he said, "Jesus Christ, let's just fucking quit this shit. For three-and-a-half weeks we've been talking about this fucking shit. Now the game's over and I'm not gonna talk about it no fucking more."

Sammy Ellis, sitting by his locker later that night, looked back over the previous few weeks and said, "I'd bet my *house* we'd be a game and a half, two games better in the standings right now if we'd just lost that damn game at the time." At the end of the season, Steinbrenner agreed, saying that the Yankees had "lost momentum" from the decision and had "never recovered." Though Steinbrenner's statement isn't exhaustively accurate—the pine-tar game was almost a month behind them when the Yankees dropped three of four to the Orioles in the crucial September series at the Stadium—one shouldn't dismiss it too glibly merely because he said it. True, the Yankees winning percentage was virtually the same before and after the game (.565 and .557, respectively), but we can get a fairer look about what it meant to their momentum by discounting the earlier part of the season and considering them from the All-Star break onward. The Yankees were 41–35 at the break; 50–36 during the second half. During the stretch between MacPhail's pine-tar decision and the August 18 replay, however, the Yankees were 8–13, for a .380 per-

< 115 >

centage. Over the rest of their second-half games, their record was 42–23, a .646 percentage. If the Yankees had played as well during those twenty-one pine-tar-obsessed games as they did for the games that surrounded them, they would have come into the season's final series still in reach of Baltimore. Steinbrenner isn't always wrong.

< 116 >

9

The Ghost of
Thurman Munson

The pine-tar slump dramatized an unfortunate truth about the 1983
Yankees: they were a leaderless team. In a certain sense, they had been
one since the death of Thurman Munson midway through the 1979
season. Munson, notoriously grumpy with outsiders, had been a driving and unifying force among his teammates. He growled at rookies
and then patted their asses, and if he felt that anyone—rookie or
veteran—wasn't giving full effort or attention to the serious business
of winning baseball games, he confronted the malingerer. His role was
particularly critical on a team where Steinbrenner's impatient readiness to shuffle players in and out of pinstripes constantly threatened
confidence and continuity. But when Munson died, there was no one
to replace him.

To occasional observers, Reggie Jackson might have seemed like a
leader, but while there is no denying his on-field effectiveness or his
willingness to deal with the press, he wasn't. Right through the end
of his Yankee career, too many of his teammates were skeptical about
his commitment to the team, doubtful that he drove even himself as
hard as he could have. "Reggie was for Reggie," said one long-time
Yankee, "and to the extent that made us winners, that was good for
him and for us. But Thurman was for the Yankees first, and if that

< 117 >

turned out to be good for him personally, that was sort of an extra thing—a bonus he hadn't counted on."

But by the time of the pine-tar slump, Jackson had been gone for a year and a half, and one might have expected Graig Nettles to assume the mantle of leadership. As Munson's—and Lou Gehrig's and Babe Ruth's—successor as Yankee captain, Nettles was playing his eleventh Yankee season; only Lou Piniella, who'd joined the club in 1974, approached him in seniority. Nettles was only the second captain to be named in more than forty years (the job had remained vacant for thirty-five years after Gehrig's death), but in his case the office did not make the man.

On the field, Nettles was an unquestioned leader. It was he who'd precipitated the pine-tar rulings, first by noticing the extra tar daubed on Brett's bat and then by putting that together with the hit that Munson had lost eight seasons earlier; he who got a critical out in a difficult game against Oakland by picking up a baserunning error and calling for an appeal play; he who regularly braved the Gossage firestorm to deliver the reminder that there were a couple of runners on base. Perhaps most important, he was one of the two or three Yankees opponents least liked to see at bat with the game on the line.

To Nettles, this *was* leadership. After the first game in the Yankees' crucial September series with Baltimore—a game he won with a late, tie-breaking home run—he said, "This is the time of year when the leaders take over, when they get the big hits, make the big plays, and pick the team up." He was right, of course, but incompletely so. Any team—but perhaps especially a team whose players had as many personal snakes and ladders as the '83 Yankees—needs clubhouse leaders as well. Martin, though undoubtedly still one of the best dugout managers in baseball, was almost brutally single-minded; if a player wasn't actively helping, he might as well not exist. After Robertson's injury removed him from the roster, for example, Martin went through the rest of the season without even telephoning him. And when Martin benched Kemp for Mattingly, the decision was communicated only by the posting of the day's lineup card. Kemp, accustomed to a different sort of managing during his previous major league years, sank deeper and deeper into a funk as he sat on the bench, and someone should have gone over and talked to him. Baylor

< 118 >

did his best, but Baylor, though a veteran, was, like Kemp, a first-year Yankee.

If there was ever a situation that cried out for intervention, this was it. Help couldn't come from the outfield coaches. Lee Walls was too much in Martin's thrall to venture across the locker room toward a player who'd landed in the manager's doghouse, and Roy White had effectively withdrawn from everything except his racing form. It almost had to come from the captain, but the thought never seemed to cross Nettles's mind. Day after day, as Kemp slipped further and further away from the point where he could turn himself around, Nettles sat in his locker, buried in one of a season-long succession of paperback mysteries. He had discovered reading during the off-season —"I never in my life read, just for the pleasure of it, before this year," he said—and had thrown himself into it so thoroughly that he often seemed not to notice any world outside the fictional one inhabited by Travis McGee.

There were, perhaps, other reasons as well why Nettles didn't reach out to Kemp, didn't call a team meeting during the pine-tar slump. Perhaps the most immediate way of creating a bond among strangers is to share a joke, and relationships as intimate as marriage often founder or float depending on the partners' ability to laugh at the same things. Even after an adult life devoted to baseball, however, Nettles didn't much share in the game's typical forms of humor.

This is, it should be noted, an observation and not a criticism, for much baseball "humor" is as unrewarding as this example of snappy repartee between Shane Rawley and Sammy Ellis from a late-season bus ride:

"Ellis, you're a piece of shit."

"*You're* a piece of shit."

"You're a *fat* piece of shit."

"You're a *skinny* piece of shit."

"You're a fat piece of shit with a twitch."

"Yeah? And you're a skinny piece of shit with a .500 record."

Not surprisingly, Nettles, a virtuoso of the verbal float-and-jab, was somewhat at a distance from such dialogues. Which dialogue was, I should add, entirely representative; one has to remember that the

< 119 >

Yankee clubhouse was a place where Sparky Lyle's habit of removing his clothes and sitting on birthday cakes was regarded as the height of wit.

Nettles's approach to cakes was somewhat different. Early in the season, Steinbrenner—whom Gossage had not inaccurately described as "the fat man"—issued an edict to the Yankee trainer that all clubhouse foods were henceforth to be "healthful and nutritious" and that, even on the road, clubhouse men would no longer be allowed to have candy bars available for the players. This rule was bendable on birthdays, however, and one, in late June, was the occasion for helium balloons and a large cake. "Oh, boy!" said Nettles, when he saw the display, "Broccoli cake! My favorite!"

Even Nettles's nickname—"Puff," short for "Puff o' smoke," a reference to the speed with which he dressed and vanished after games —made it clear that his was hardly a dominant clubhouse presence. Perhaps it was just not in his personality to be one, or perhaps he felt that as long as he gave of himself so thoroughly on the field locker-room leadership was simply not his job. Late in the season, during the Yankees' final series at Fenway, I asked him what he thought it meant to be the sixth captain in Yankee history. "Nobody ever told me what it meant," he said. "Not the manager, not the owner, not anyone. So I don't know what the job specifically is. I guess it's like an honor or something, and that's it. I was never paid any extra for it, and was never told what the duties were, except to take the lineup card out, so I just go along the same way I always have."

Given the size of Nettles's locker, which let him set a folding chair up inside it, a visitor to the Yankee clubhouse could pass through the locker room without noticing his presence. This is something no one could ever say about Oscar Gamble. Loud, vulgar, and unfailingly cheerful, Gamble was the chief Yankee needler, and as one of the few players willing or able to break the tension that sometimes gripped the team, he played an invaluable role. Early in August, when Cerone was at his most depressed and withdrawn, for instance, and so preoc-cupied with the trade rumors surrounding him that he was barely going through the motions during batting practice, Gamble quickly noticed and got on him. "Oooh, Ricky! Another pop-up. All them

< 120 >

scouts from Los Angeles sittin' up there watchin' you. . . . Oh, oh. Another pop-up. One more, you gonna be sittin' on Tommy Lasorda's bench, too."

Cerone grinned over at him briefly, seemed almost visibly to concentrate, then drove a hard liner to left field. "Fuck you, Oscar," he said triumphantly.

"Okay, you got the Padres interested in you now. You want to go to the Padres, or the Series? Gotta do that *all* the time for L.A." Cerone finished his turn with two more solidly hit balls, then came out of the cage. On the way past Gamble, he thanked him with a wordless pat.

Early in the season, Gamble had had plenty of help in his important task; Murcer, Piniella, and Rudy May were pretty ready with the needle themselves. But Murcer made way for Mattingly in June, Piniella grew increasingly preoccupied by the recurring dizziness that was keeping him out of the late-season lineup and backed away from his needler's role, May spent a large chunk of the season on the disabled list and virtually all of it on Martin's shit list, and Gamble was left virtually alone. Without anybody to pick up his comments and elaborate on them, to validate them as jokes by building them into baroque fantasies that eventually collapsed in laughter, Gamble's opening assaults often sounded simply shrill and mean, and they vanished in the electricity-laden air of the clubhouse before they could do any good.

Though he kept trying, his efforts were further complicated by his gradually diminishing role with the team. Baylor's strong season, and his ability to hit right-handers, cut into Gamble's playing time, and perhaps as a frustrated reaction—this was the final year of his Yankee contract, and the size of his next deal depended on his ability to put some numbers on the board—his performance tailed off badly as the season wore on. On July 1, he was batting .304 with five home runs, but he added only one homer in July and another in August and by September 1 his average had dwindled to .279. For the rest of the season, he hit .154 with no homers and no r.b.i.'s, and wound up with a batting average that had shrunk to .261. As a consequence, the Yankees were without an effective class clown at the stomach-tightening time when they most needed one. "It's hard to explain why," said

< 121 >

one veteran, "but things just *sound* different when they're coming from a guy who's sitting on the bench."

Among the remaining Yankee veterans, Willie Randolph was in many ways the least likely candidate for a leadership role. Brooding, intense, and as quiet as Gamble was loud, he often seemed more preoccupied with individual goals than with the team's performance. After one late August game during which the Yankees had signaled their emergence from the pine-tar torpor with a come-from-behind victory over California, Randolph's was the only unsmiling face in the locker room. He was upset because his bad-hop grounder had been scored as an error, depriving him of a game-winning r.b.i., and he was scathingly angry that earlier he'd been charged with an error for failing to handle an off-line throw on what might have been a double play.

This sort of petulance wasn't at all unusual for Randolph, and his usefulness to the 1983 Yankees was further limited by injuries that kept him out of 58 games. A nagging hamstring twice put him on the disabled list, an injury to his right knee cut short an early-season road trip, and he sat out several more games with a whiplashed neck. His 104 games-played was his lowest total (except for the strike-shortened season) in eight years as a Yankee, and some of the players had privately questioned the seriousness of his neck injury.

And yet when one talked to younger Yankees—Robertson, Meacham, Dayett—they universally volunteered that it had been Randolph, among all the veterans, who had reached out toward them and made them feel welcomed to the team. He'd also been the first—and remained the most regular—Yankee to visit Robertson in the hospital after his auto accident, and it sometimes seemed as though there were two different Willie Randolphs wearing pinstripes.

A couple of times during the season, when I'd tried to talk with him about this, Randolph had been almost rudely incommunicative, but one rainy September afternoon, when he learned that one of my sons had recently graduated from a Brooklyn high school that had been among his high school rivals, he grabbed a chair for me and began talking. Randolph's speaking style, like his play, was quick, deft, and certain, and he addressed the subject of his conflicting images almost as though he'd been thinking about the answers for a while and had merely been waiting for the question. "I think a lot of people fail to

< 122 >

understand me," he said, "or even to know me. I'm not a very contro-versial or flamboyant person, but I can't help noticing that a lot of writers—and it's only through the writers that the fans get to know your personality—don't just come up to me and talk. Instead, they tend to go to other people for second-hand information.

"There are reasons for that," he continued, "but the reasons are history, and you would think they'd be done by now. I don't really need the recognition or attention, but I don't like what comes across about me as a person. There's a lot of taking shots about a person's personality or moods, but everybody has their moods."

Well, sure. But why did he think writers distorted *his* personality? He began, appropriately, at the beginning, with his introduction to organized baseball. "There was a bunch of us kids used to play ball on the grass in front of the projects," he said, talking about Tilden Houses, in the Brownsville section of Brooklyn. "In those olden times," he grinned, "you weren't allowed to play on the grass, and the gardener used to come chase us off three or four times a day. Eventu-ally, I guess, he got tired of writing us up and screaming at us, and he said, 'Either I'm gonna have you put in jail or you can meet me at Prospect Park, and I'll teach you the right way to play the game.' It turned out he'd been a minor league ballplayer, and he really could teach us. He got me into the Puerto Rican League, and when I was eleven or twelve I made the All-Star team and we went to Puerto Rico to play some games down there."

It was then that Randolph first began to see baseball as his ticket out of the housing projects, out of Brownsville. He played as much as he could: Pony League, American Legion ball "with a tough old Spanish manager," and Tilden High, where the scouts began taking a serious look at him. He was a shortstop then, and "always the smallest kid on every team. A little guy, but I was always batting third, never hitting less than three and change." When the Pirates offered him a contract, he took it without hesitation. "I gave myself five years in the minor leagues. If I didn't make it by then, I was going to go back to school, get a degree, and maybe coach." Late in the 1975 season, after only two and a half years, he made it to the parent organization when Rennie Stennett got hurt. He still remembers his playoff debut: "I was shaking in my shoes, I was so nervous, and when Danny Murtaugh said, 'Hey, son, grab a bat,' I didn't know if I was

< 123 >

going to be able to climb out of the dugout. Don Gullett was pitching for Cincinnati, throwing about ninety-five plus, and I struck out and *ran* back to the dugout."

After that season, he was traded to the Yankees, where Martin was beginning his own first full season as Yankee manager. Randolph had a good spring, winning the Dawson award as the camp's outstanding rookie, but he was still only twenty-two years old, and desperately unsure of himself. "It was too crowded, too much going on, no privacy at all. Plus," he recalled, "I was a very serious young man—this was how I was going to make my living—and the Yankees were a different kind of team from the Pirates. There was no Willie Stargell or anything like that. You know," he smiled at the memory, "he'd *hug* you when you did something good.

"So I just kept to myself. Got dressed, played the games, and went home. Now we'll get to what I meant by 'history.' At that time, there were no black writers covering us at all—and there's only one now, you'll notice—and mostly old guys. I think they took my shyness wrong, figured me as some kind of militant or something. If I was a white kid, they could have seen it, would have said, 'He's serious' or 'He's shy,' but what they said instead was, 'He's sullen.'

"And maybe, if it had gone on that way for longer, I would have been, but you know who turned things around? Thurman Munson. He came over to my locker one day—I wouldn't have dared to walk to his—and he tossed me this package. 'There you are, kid,' he said, 'Open it up.' It was a T-shirt, this *loud* yellow and green, and on the front it said 'Rook.' I must've worn that under my uniform almost every day, and I've still got it at home in my drawer. It's ratty now, all full of holes, but I would *never* throw it away."

"And so," he continued, "to tell the truth, I try to make all the youngsters who come here feel welcome. Pat 'em on the back, shake their hands, especially if they've had a down game. I've been back there in that time, and Willie Stargell and Thurman were really super to me. I spent a lot of time with Meacham and Robertson this year, because I learned from those two guys that if I don't make you feel comfortable, I'm not being the best I can be."

When Randolph took on some of the leadership responsibilities accruing to his seniority, he was making a conscious effort of will—just as

< 124 >

Nettles's curious passivity was a chosen path. Dave Winfield, elected by the players as team representative (the rough equivalent of shop steward), was both a statutory leader and a genuinely natural one. "I've got the body," he said one night as the season drew to an end, "I've got the strength, I've got the stamina, *and*—maybe 'therefore' —I've got the charisma."

He wasn't exaggerating, and his "therefore" was right. The main reason so many people have remarked about Ralph Houk's being a leader on the great Yankee teams of the early fifties was that his marginal status as a third-string catcher made him a striking exception in that role. Ballplayers—who have so much of it that they don't have to be defensive about where theirs ends—respect talent, and most of the Yankees were at least occasionally in awe of Winfield. Even among the exceptionally gifted group of athletes that made up the Yankees, he stood alone.

Physically, he dwarfed his teammates. At six feet one inch and 210 pounds, Don Baylor is among the bigger ballplayers in the league, with more than enough power to jerk the ball over the Stadium's distant left-field wall. Winfield is five full inches taller, and fifteen to twenty pounds heavier. He is, if you can imagine such a thing, bigger than Baylor by more than twice the margin that Baylor is bigger than Willie Randolph.

And he is perhaps uniquely gifted. As a star outfielder at the University of Minnesota, he batted over .400 and was MVP in the 1973 College World Series. But in his senior year, he also pitched, and in the extremely competitive Big 10 Conference he compiled a 13–1 record. In basketball, after his intramural team, "the Soulful Strutters," destroyed the university's junior varsity, he was prevailed upon to try out for the varsity. "On the first day," he remembered, "they were *embarrassing* me, so every day from then on, I'm determined not to let that happen again. In a very short time period, I went from a walk-on to a starter." For his work with Minnesota's "Iron Five," he was drafted by the Atlanta Hawks of the NBA and the Utah Stars of the ABA. The Minnesota Vikings also drafted him as a potential professional football player. After graduation, though, he signed with the San Diego Padres, and went directly from the campus to the major leagues. Even now, when many southern and western colleges play hundred-game schedules, such a leap is rare in the extreme; ten years

< 125 >

ago, it was unprecedented. Among the 1983 Yankees, Cerone, Kemp, and Smalley were all experienced college players and first-round draft choices, but each of them played at least one full season in the minors before getting a look at big league pitching. Winfield came right up and hit a solid .277.

Fully aware of his role and responsibility as a team leader, Winfield described that role in very specific terms: "There's no 'rah-rah' in it at all. The season is too long, and the players—including the guys on the other teams—are too professional. A couple of times, though it hasn't been so bad this year, when George has come into the clubhouse and given us 'Win one for the Gipper,' it's been embarrassing. What *I* am, as a leader, is," he paused and searched for the accurate phrase, "an influential peer.

"That means," he continued, "that when I'm hot, I can change the behavior and attitude of the players around me. Take that Detroit series, when everything I hit was *flying*. I mean, I still get excited every time I look at those films. Now imagine that I'm hitting the ball like that, we're two runs down going into the ninth, and I'm fourth or fifth up—even sixth. Are the guys in front of me going to give up? No. They're gonna go up there saying to themselves, 'If I can do something—work a walk, get on base, keep us alive somehow—we're gonna win this thing.' And they're *right* to believe that. That kind of leadership isn't done with mirrors or anything; it's *real*. I can't do it all the time—nobody can—and if I don't there are a lot of other players on this team who can play that role for at least a little while. But I *do* have to do it more often than anyone else. That's what I'm paid for, that's what my job is."

How about his role as player rep? When the team was reeling during the pine-tar days, he was holding regular player meetings. Should he—should the team—have handled things differently? "Looking back, you can certainly say that maybe we should have said, 'Of course we'll play the rest of the game. We'll play it any time, anywhere, and we'll win—same as we would've if we'd finished the game that day.' But," he added, "you have to remember that it wasn't only the players who had something to say about the game. There was a total response, from the total Yankee organization—including the owner.

"I don't say everything George does is right—I've taken the man

< 126 >

to court over my contract once already—but there are some things he's *entitled* to. When he's out there, fighting for us as hard as he can according to what he thinks is right—and I hear he's gonna be fined again for some of the stuff he said—you have to coordinate your response to his. The man who pays the salaries has got *some* rights."

Feeling that way, couldn't he have gone into those endless "will we play–won't we play?" meetings and said, "Listen, I know this is a charade, but . . ."? "No," he said without any hesitation. "In the first place, we *needed* that day off. My knees were voting not to play, I'll tell you that. And," he grinned, "if I had said something like that, how long would it take before you guys found out about it and Lee Mac-Phail was reading in the papers that the team was walking away from George? With this organization, there are too many actors for anyone to go off by himself."

It's hard to say that there is anything wrong with Winfield's notion of leadership, and impossible to say that he didn't live up to it. He played hurt—after almost every game, there was a half-dollar-sized circle of blood where he'd once again ripped open a scab on his left knee, and all season long his strained thumb was causing him to lose his bat; he played hard—diving after uncatchable line drives, he occasionally played a single into a triple but more often turned them into outs—and he played often, if anything, too often for a lanky thirty-one-year-old whose knees absorbed a terrible beating in the great spaces of the Stadium's left field. But as he suggested, *someone* "should have said, 'Of course we'll play the rest of the game.' . . ." He was the only one who could perhaps have pulled it off, and he didn't try. The limited concept of leadership, though not wrong, turned out to have been incomplete.

It was incomplete for precisely the reason that it had come into being: the nature of the organization. In Chicago, after he had called a meeting with the players to talk about MacPhail's recent ruling, Martin derided the notion of "team leaders." "I called a meeting because that's the way I do it," he said. "I don't care if it's supposed to be the manager's job, it's *my* job. Philadelphia's got three 'team leaders' and what did they accomplish? They went behind his back and got the manager fired. And that's when they were in first place. There's a chain—owner, general manager, manager, coaches, players

< 127 >

—and that's the way it's gotta be. If you don't have that, you've got a circus."

True, perhaps, but the Yankees didn't quite have that. At any number of times during Steinbrenner's reign, the chain had been fractured from the top down. One of Martin's values, as Winfield had suggested in spring training, was that he was independent enough to deflect some of the owner's outbursts and disruptions and absorb them himself. But even Martin, as had been dramatized several times during his career, served at Steinbrenner's pleasure, and while he could take a great deal of heat about his between-the-lines decisions (his commitment to playing Nettles, for instance) he protected his own turf by being exquisitely careful not to interfere with what he regarded as an owner's or general manager's legitimate prerogatives. When disruption came from the top in the guise of *policy,* only player leadership could be a countervailing force. In 1983, it wasn't.

< 128 >

10

A Stadium Full of Steinbrenners

Despite the pine-tar slump, the Yankees were still in the race as September came around. After finishing the final four outs of the pine-tar game, they went on a 14–6 (.700) streak, winding up a long 9–4 road trip by splitting a four-game series with Milwaukee, a club which had by far the best home record in the division. But that split, which they salvaged by taking the final two games, was costly, for Gossage worked on both days, throwing a total of 65 pitches. With the Yankees in sole possession of second, five games behind Baltimore, their next home series—four games in three days against the Orioles —was critical, but Gossage was definitely unavailable for the first game, and perhaps for the next day's doubleheader as well.

In the locker room after the final Milwaukee game, Gossage admitted he'd "have preferred not to pitch tonight," but added that "in September, you do what you gotta do. It's no-bullshit time now. We just gotta kick the shit out of 'em in New York." The Yankees were looking forward to the prospect—not necessarily of *doing* it but of being in a position to try. A few days earlier, in Seattle, Roy Smalley had said that for the first time in his professional career he "was having fun in August and September." And the fact of being in a pennant race after seasons of playing out the string with Minnesota

< 129 >

seemed to have lifted his game. Thrust back into the starting short-stop's role after Robertson's injury, Smalley had played one disastrous defensive game during the trip—two ninth-inning errors that cost the Yankees a win against California—but he'd also hit .341 and driven in 10 runs over the 13-game stretch. Eager as he was, however, an as-yet-undiagnosed problem had afflicted him with a dizziness so severe he'd had to come out of the final Milwaukee game early. He claimed he was ready to play, though, for no one wanted to miss the season's biggest series. As George Steinbrenner, who'd come out for the end of the road trip, said in the Milwaukee visitors' locker room, "This team has surprised me; they've shown a lot of character. There are maybe fourteen thousand things that could go wrong, and they all have, but they're still in it. Now we'll see what they're made of, 'cause their backs are really up against the wall."

For all that his remarks showed an inordinate fondness for sports cliché, Steinbrenner was right. The Yankees had not only weathered the curse-in-disguise of the pine-tar victory, they had survived a pain-fully slow start, a benchful of bruised egos, and a flock of injuries. Now, facing a series that couldn't win them the pennant—but that could knock them from the race—the slow start was forgotten, and the bruised egos subsumed into the team's collective personality.

Only the injuries remained unyielding. Three weeks after Robert-son's season-ending traffic accident, the Yankees had suffered their second freak loss of the season, when Steve Kemp was hit by a batting-practice liner from Omar Moreno. His cheekbone shattered and the prospect of eye surgery likely, Kemp remained in a Mil-waukee hospital while his teammates flew home. There were nagging injuries as well, which Steinbrenner, typically, wanted to blame on *someone;* and on the plane to New York, he cornered Yankee trainer Gene Monahan and began complaining about the team's physician, Dr. Joseph Bonomo. "I got Piniella getting no better, I got Wynegar getting no better. I don't care if he's got *twenty* operations tomorrow; I want him out to the ballpark by three or four o'clock tomorrow, when we get there, or he's *through* with us. We pay him a helluva lot of money and at least he ought to *be* there."

By game time, all were present and accounted for. Piniella was still unable to look up for fly balls without dizziness but had taken batting practice and announced himself available for pinch-hitting; Smalley,

< 130 >

also still subject to dizziness, was in the starting lineup. "It's one of those 'it only hurts when I laugh' things," he said. "The only time it really bothers me is when I get tired going around the bases, and I just hope I get a chance to get real tired tonight." Wynegar, still nagged by an injury that prevented him from batting right-handed, was on the bench against Oriole lefty Scott McGregor, as was, somewhat more surprisingly, the slumping Cerone, whose place had been taken by rookie Juan Espino. Another rookie, Don Mattingly, was a late sub for Piniella in right.

The Oriole lineup featured, as it had all year against left-handers like Guidry, the right-handed outfield platoon: Gary Roenicke in left, John Shelby in center, and Dan Ford in right. The Orioles' switch-hitting regulars, first baseman Eddie Murray and dh Ken Singleton, were also turned around against Guidry, so at least some of the O's usual power would probably be blunted by the vast acreage in the Stadium's left field. The 40,000-plus crowd roundly booed all these players as they were announced and roared encouragement for the Yankees. For the first time during the season, the Stadium had the electric, "big game" feeling that marks a tight pennant race. The previous five months had been a war of attrition, a gradual accumulation of wins and losses that had given the O's their lead but no one of which had mattered *individually*. Big games are those that not only matter in the standings but are psychologically decisive as well.

The Orioles started off in their classic aggressive mode. Leadoff batter John Shelby drove Guidry's first pitch on a line to left field, but Winfield was waiting for it. Dan Ford, however, went the other way, and banged a double off the right-center wall. With Cal Ripkin and Eddie Murray, the O's MVP candidates, coming up, Baltimore was in a good position to take an early lead, adding significantly to the pressure the standings already were putting on the Yankees. They were certainly going for it, as, with the count 2–2 on Ripkin, Ford broke for third. Ripkin fouled it off, however, and two pitches later, admired a Guidry slider for a called strike three. When Murray hit Guidry's first pitch hard, but to Moreno, the Yankees escaped.

The Yankees started off even stronger in their half of the first. After Willie Randolph slapped a single to left, number-two batter Ken Griffey, normally not a home run hitter, waited nicely on a McGregor

< 131 >

curve and sent it over the right-field fence to give the Yankees a 2–0 lead.

The Orioles got one run back right away when, with two on and two out, Rick Dempsey fought off a change and a fastball in, squibbing fouls, then hit a clean r.b.i. single to right. Guidry got out of the inning without further harm, though, when Shelby grounded out to first.

After that, both pitchers settled down. The Yankees wasted Mattingly's leadoff double in the second when McGregor, working the outside of the plate, struck out both Espino and Moreno; but they added a run in the fifth on Winfield's two-out double, to take a 3–1 lead. Guidry, meanwhile, was cruising. He wasn't piling up the strikeouts—the Orioles are an aggressive club at the plate, ready to go the opposite way on pitches that other teams might let go by—but he was getting the outs. From the third through seventh innings, no Oriole runner advanced beyond first, and—an important side effect of their aggressiveness, given the state of the Yankee bullpen—Guidry completed the seventh having thrown only 92 pitches, well under his usual average.

He retired the side on only nine in the top of the eighth, but since these nine pitches included a first-pitch single by Ripkin (an easy double if Winfield hadn't played it perfectly as it flew back off the wall) and a first-pitch home run into the left-field seats from Roenicke, the O's had tied the game at 3. This was precisely the sort of thing the Orioles had been doing all year, so the rally couldn't have come as a surprise to the fans, but it surely quieted them down.

Baylor immediately livened them up, though, leading off the home eighth with an infield single deep into the hole, and as Nettles came to the plate the cowbell-and-whistle brigade was hard at it in the right-field bleachers. Tippy Martinez had started to work in the Orioles' bullpen, but, after a visit to the mound from the O's pitching coach, McGregor stayed in. Historically, he'd been tough on Nettles, and though Nettles had already had two doubles off him in this game, he'd struck out once, and the second double had been accidental—an inside pitch that Nettles had tried to avoid but had wound up blooping just inside the left-field foul line. Playing the percentages, Nettles squared to bunt but let the first pitch go by for a strike. The next two broke outside, but when another pitch grazed the outside black for the

< 132 >

second strike, the bunt option was removed. McGregor's fifth pitch was head high, also well out of the strike zone, but in over the plate, and Nettles got all of it, driving it deep into the right-field grandstand on a line. The Stadium exploded into sound as the ball left the bat, and the roar continued through Nettles's home run trot, calming only after he'd come out of the dugout for a curtain call. When Smalley followed the home run with his second single of the night, McGregor was gone.

Smalley was gone as well, for a pinch runner. This was partly owing to his illness—Martin didn't want a baserunner who might fall down trying to get an extra base—but was also consistent with the manager's pattern of bringing in a defensive substitute for Smalley when the Yankees had a late-inning lead. The tactic had occasionally blown up in Martin's face (Bobby Meacham's Milwaukee boot, for example), but it was hard to argue that it was wrong.

Pinch runner Otis Nixon drew four pickoff throws from reliever Tippy Martinez, then broke for second on the first pitch home, reaching it easily when Mattingly dropped a sacrifice bunt. With one out and a runner in scoring position, Piniella pinch-hit for Espino. This was the ailing Piniella's first trip to the plate since August 23, when he'd popped out, and he'd been hitless since August 2. Against Martinez, he was totally overmatched; unable to pick up the spin on the ball, he waved at three pitches, then sat down. Perhaps sensing that they were seeing Piniella for the last time, and undoubtedly put in a mood by Nettles's homer to cheer *anything,* the Stadium crowd rose and gave him a standing ovation as he trudged back toward the dugout. Moreno also struck out, to no applause, but even against Baltimore, and even with Guidry perhaps beginning to tire, a two-run lead going into the ninth inning didn't look bad at all.

It started to look shaky, however, when Martin's tactic once again backfired; Larry Milbourne, in for Smalley, misplayed Dauer's easy grounder, and the leadoff batter reached base. With May and Frazier throwing in the Yankee bullpen, pinch hitter Benny Ayala hit another grounder to Milbourne, who this time handled it perfectly, turning a 6-4-3 double play. Guidry got the final out on a routine fly to Winfield, and the Yankees had moved to four games out of first.

They'd done it, it should be remarked, in a hugely entertaining game. Though the totals wound up showing eighteen hits and eight

< 133 >

runs, the middle five innings had provided the fans with a genuine pitchers' duel. There had been clutch hitting from each team and a couple of solid defensive plays, and the errors—which provided a necessary element of chance—had turned out to be meaningless. Nettles, an aging hero, had performed precisely the way aging heroes are supposed to, and—at least in this sense, "thanks" to Milbourne's error—Guidry had needed to face the tying run in the ninth inning. Though the game had hardly been a classic, it had taken the New York fans for a splendid roller-coaster ride—the early up, the sudden drop, and equally sudden euphoria, and a final frisson of tension had made the night *fun*.

In his office after the game, Martin seemed to find less pleasure in the win itself than in the private vindication it provided him, saying, "Remember back in spring training, when you guys kept writing the only reason Nettles was playing was because he's my friend? Well, I guess it's a good thing he likes me, or he wouldn't be here."

Nettles, with somewhat more excuse, played a variation on the theme: "Well," he laughed, "I'm glad I have a friend in the manager's office." More seriously, he added, "I think I'm proving something with every game I play. It wasn't just the writers, or even the people the writers talk to," he rolled his eyes heavenward toward the Yankee executive offices, "but a lot of people didn't expect me to play, a lot of people expected me to fold in the dog days. It gives me a lot of pleasure to prove those people were wrong."

Was his performance, then, just a victory for personal pride? "No, but don't get me wrong. I think pride matters. It used to be a guy could maybe double his salary from postseason play, but now it's really the pride part you play for. You want people to look at you all winter and say, 'There goes a winner.' That's why at this time of year, on good teams, you see the good players take over to lead the team, carry it. We've got a lot of guys who can play that role for us."

So, of course, did Baltimore, and if the Yankee locker room seemed considerably less euphoric than the stands had been, it had less to do with Martin's I-told-you-so bitterness than with the players' realistic assessment of their chances. Asked about the four-game sweep at Fenway in 1978, Nettles unhesitatingly said, "That was different. We were facing a team that was on its way downhill, but this team is on the way up. They're hot, and it doesn't seem like they ever lose two

< 134 >

or three in a row. That's why three out of four is realistically what you look for here, and you just hope for a sweep. It's hard to win a doubleheader, even against a team that's not as good as they are, and that's what makes a sweep so tough.

"This was a good game to win, though. With the standings the way they are, I don't think we can afford a split, and winning the first one really helps. You know, we were drained from the long road trip and the late night last night, and they had yesterday off. So I'm sure they felt physically better than we did, and if they'd won tonight, then the pressure on us tomorrow would have been really a *lot* to handle. Now, we can just go out and play."

In his office, before Saturday's twi-nighter, Martin was unusually relaxed. He had, it's true, dissipated some of his tensions by chewing out Tom Boswell of the *Washington Post* for asking why the Yankees had played Espino rather than Cerone, but he was also able to laugh at himself. Watching the tail end of a Cubs-Cardinals game on television, he winced at an error, then grinned, "It's *amazing* how much easier it is to watch something like that from in here. If I was on the bench and that was our guys out there, my stomach would be hurting now."

Between innings, he passed around a picture of his son, Billy Joe, who had just begun college that week. "That's his girlfriend in the picture with him," said Martin. "A nice girl too. I'm real proud of him."

He was pulled back into Yankee baseball, at least briefly, when Walls brought in Brian Dayett, whose contract the Yankees had just purchased from Columbus. Martin stood up to shake the rookie's hand, and told Walls to take Dayett down to the batting cage under the stands for some hitting. After they'd gone, he said, "We need that right-handed bat bad right now. I would have used him last night if I'd had him. Lou wanted to try, and maybe he could do it in the daylight, but last night he couldn't see the ball *at all.* He was hittin' okay in batting practice, but there you don't have to worry about picking up the spin. He got up there against Martinez and had no idea what the pitch was gonna do."

Facing young Storm Davis in the sun of a late September afternoon, the Yankees certainly seemed to have little difficulty seeing the ball.

< 135 >

They moved to a 2–0 lead with only one out in the second, as Mattingly scored from second on an off-line Shelby throw and Wynegar, who'd singled him home, crossed on Moreno's double. With Yankee runners on second and third and only one out, the Baltimore bullpen was busy as the pitching coach walked toward the mound. Davis toughened up, though, and got two quick strikes on Randolph. But Randolph is a superlative contact hitter, and he fouled off three tough pitches as he worked the count to 2–2. Then he drove a bullet on the ground, right at Eddie Murray, who made the putout unassisted. The ball was hit so hard that Smalley couldn't advance, and when Davis struck out Griffey, the threat of a big inning evaporated. The Yankees continued to knock on the door, getting runners into scoring position in each of their next three times at bat, only to have Davis close it in their faces each time.

Meanwhile, aided by a nice 6–4–3 double play started from deep in the hole by Smalley, Rawley set Baltimore down in order through the first three innings. In the fourth and fifth, the O's started to threaten, but Rawley's timely strikeouts preserved his shutout, and the O's twice left two men on base. In the sixth, however, it appeared that Rawley had been working a little too close to the horns and that he was about to get gored. He opened the inning with a walk, a single, and a fly that advanced the lead runner. But with runners at first and third and only one out, Rawley continued his mastery of Roenicke, getting the left fielder to hit his second double-play ball of the game. This time, however, Smalley's throw to Randolph was well off line, and by the time Randolph turned and got the ball to first, both runners were safe and Ford had crossed the plate. Instead of the Yankees closing out the inning with a 2–0 lead, it was 2–1, and there were still two runners on and only one out. Designated hitter Ken Singleton worked the count to 3–2, then, with both runners going, swung and missed, and Wynegar's throw to third completed the double play. The Orioles shouldn't have scored at all—their one run was unearned—but the Yankees, having given them the equivalent of five outs, were lucky to hold them that low.

The Orioles tied the score an inning later, legitimately, on another walk, a sac bunt, and Dempsey's double to center. With the leading run in scoring position, however, Rawley struck out Shelby for the second time and got Ford on a routine grounder to Randolph.

< 136 >

At the same time that Baltimore had begun first to threaten and then to score, the Yankee bats had dried up. Davis, who'd thrown a lot of pitches, departed at the end of the fifth inning, and Sammy Stewart came on to start the fourth tour through the Yankee batting order. Through the sixth, seventh, and eighth, he held the Yankees to one hit, a meaningless single from Nettles. The O's also failed to score in the eighth, and as the two teams entered the ninth they were matched at two runs, six hits and one error each—with each of the errors responsible for a run.

In the ninth, however, the Stadium fell in on the Yankees. Rawley, still pitching strongly, got a grounder to short from leadoff Lenn Sakata. Smalley gloved the ball, set, and threw it so far over Griffey's head that it caromed back on to the field too quickly for even the speedy Sakata to try for second. Cruz moved him over with his second sacrifice bunt, though, and Martin called for the Goose to pitch for Dempsey.

Though Rawley didn't appear to be tiring, and though the 119 pitches he'd thrown were well within his usual limit of effectiveness, bringing in Gossage wasn't the sort of decision most grandstand managers would have second-guessed. The score is tied in the ninth, a runner is in scoring position, your starter is facing a guy who doubled off him last time up, and you have one of the best relief pitchers in baseball throwing in your bullpen. If you don't use him *then,* what can you possibly be saving him for? Throughout the season, however, Martin had tended to stick with his starters until they had gotten themselves into deeper trouble, so the decision to go with the Goose was uncharacteristically safe.

Gossage certainly came in as though he meant business, throwing two quick strikes to Dempsey, but losing him on a walk. First and second, one out. Then, with Gossage in and no left-hander throwing in the Yankee bullpen, Altobelli began inserting his left-handed batters. Reserve catcher Joe Nolan batted for Shelby, and he too fell behind 0–2 on a couple of sizzling fastballs. Despite a scouting report indicating that Nolan was vulnerable to breaking stuff, the next four pitches were pure heat as well—all of them either strikes or too close to the plate to risk taking at 0–2. Four times, Nolan fouled off Gossage heaters, each time getting a better look at the ball as he grew more used to its pace. When he saw his seventh straight fastball, he smacked

< 137 >

it on a line to left center, scoring the lead runner: 3–2, runners on first and second, one out. Gossage got the second out on an infield fly, but Cal Ripkin lined a double to right, scoring Dempsey; Landrum, pinch-running for Nolan, held at third on Mattingly's strong throw; and the Orioles led, 4–2, runners on second and third, two out, with cleanup hitter Eddie Murray coming to bat.

Here, the book called for an intentional walk, bypassing Murray and setting up a play at any base. The traditional percentages were, however, offset in this case by the near certainty that Baltimore's shift to its left-handed platoon would bring John Lowenstein up as a pinch hitter after Murray. In talking about this series a week earlier in Seattle, Martin had stressed the importance of his left-handed starters being able to "keep Lowenstein out of the lineup." Adding his respect for Lowenstein to his well-known predilection for managing *against* the book, one might have expected Martin to have Gossage take his chances with Murray. But for the second time that inning, Martin chose the "safe" option and gave the sign for an intentional walk.

As is by now well known, the strategy backfired spectacularly. Lowenstein hit the first pitch over the right-center-field wall for a grand-slam home run, and the Orioles had an insurmountable 8–2 lead.

That ninth inning was undoubtedly a painful one for Yankee fans, and I suspect that many of them, years from now, will still "see" Lowenstein's home run with the same pain-honed sharpness that I see Bucky Dent's blooped home run clearing the wall at Fenway during the 1978 playoff. But the season-record crowd of 55,605 were more than disappointed; they were bitter, even angry—and, perhaps because they'd already gotten a night's drinking in, boorish. They greeted the announcement of Smalley's name in the second-game lineup with a rolling thunder of jeers, and many of those within screaming range of the Yankee bullpen furiously cursed Gossage on his way to the outfield bench. Their attitude seemed to be that the Yankees should have won—should, indeed, win all the crucial games —and they acted not so much let down as betrayed.

This behavior was stupid and silly—were there really any of them who thought that Gossage *wanted* to give up the home run? that Smalley *deliberately* threw the ball away?—and it raised the question of whether Yankee fans are like other fans only more so, or whether

< 138 >

there is something uniquely awful about them. In *The Bill James Baseball Abstract* for 1983, James casts his vote for the latter alternative. In the "other park characteristics" section of his discussion of stadiums, he makes note, for example, that in Baltimore "high concrete walls slanting across the outfield ricochet everything toward center. . . ." In Arlington, Texas, it's the winds, and in Oakland it's the foul territory. In Yankee Stadium, James notes only "dangerous people."

This perhaps overstates the case (James *is* from Kansas City, after all), for on any given night the people inside the Stadium are surely no more dangerous than those outside it. But they are on average as vicious and obnoxious an assemblage as you will find anywhere in the major leagues (including the notorious Chicago White Sox fans and Philadelphia Phillies fans), and it's interesting to try to figure out why.

(A brief pause here for a definition of "vicious and obnoxious." I am not referring simply to the cascades of ill-considered booing, nor even to the fondness for scatological comment from the general-admission sections, but to an overall atmosphere of alcoholic, bullying nastiness exemplified by the following vignette from an August game against Oakland.

The upper deck, along the third-base side, seemed mostly given over to well-muscled but flab-bellied young men whose matted hair was of a length that once denoted pacific hippiedom and now seems to signal residence in industrial New Jersey. They didn't have sole possession of the area, however, and in front of one such group sat a well-dressed couple—presumably married; they each wore rings—who were rooting for the A's. The woman, indeed, was wearing a green-and-yellow Oakland cap. Along about the fifth inning, with the Yankees trailing by six runs, the Stadium regulars began to vent their frustration on her. "Hey, cunt," their leader shouted to approving laughter, "Whyntcha take that fuckin' hat off?"

This went on for a while, and when her husband finally turned around to ask them to stop, his request was greeted with "Shut up, faggot." For the next two innings, until the couple finally got up and left, the gang of louts, quasi-surreptitiously supplementing their beers with swallows from smuggled half-pints of liquor, carried on a loud debate about whether or not they should kick the shit out of that fucking faggot.

< 139 >

That is what I mean by "vicious and obnoxious.")

New York itself is not to blame, nor even the fact that many of the Stadium fans arrive in a filthy mood from having ridden on a jammed, overheated, and equally filthy subway car. Shea Stadium is in New York, and though the Flushing line is marginally preferable to the Lexington Avenue trains, Mets games start a half-hour earlier than Yankee games and the subways are proportionately more crowded. One contributing factor, I suppose, is that the difference in the sizes of the teams' crowds encourages potentially obnoxious fans to feel more anonymous at Yankee Stadium than at Shea. A second, and not insignificant factor, is that Shea looks and feels like one of those suburban stadiums plunked down on the outskirts of Dallas or Houston. It is an island in a sea of parking lots. Yankee Stadium is bordered by streets with people on them, and commercial establishments—most notably two or three bars that cater almost exclusively to Yankee fans. Between them, these bars do a thriving pregame business with several hundred fans who thus manage to enter the Stadium already pretty buzzed. Under a different set of geographical circumstances, the logistics of getting a beer at a baseball game—either waiting in interminable lines at a stand or waiting almost as long for a vendor to appear—might keep the fans more sober, and hence less eager to strut their stuff.

But while those differences are real, I think the crucial ones lie somewhere in the nature of fandom. A fan's relationship with his or her team may be stable—most fans form their loyalties early and stay bound to their team until death, or the movement of the franchise, do them part—but it is hardly calm. True fans live and die with, or perhaps even through, their team. They cheer their favorites, second-guess the managers, and work countless mental trades during the off-season. The roots of this passion may be obscure, but its reality is not to be doubted. Devoted and faithful as fans may be, however, their love is not all-forgiving.

I know this at least partly because I've been a Red Sox rooter since 1946, and though I've forgiven a great deal over the intervening decades (Red Sox fans have a lot of occasions to practice this virtue), I haven't forgiven *everything*.

I was, for instance, only six years old in my first year of real fandom (*real* fans, by this definition, read the agate), and the Red Sox lost the

< 140 >

first World Series I can remember when Enos Slaughter charged all the way home from first while Johnny Pesky pondered what to do with the ball. During this year's Yankee season, I heard for the first time a story about Pesky and that famous blunder: It seems that about a month or so after the game, when Pesky finally came out of hiding, he anonymously attended a college football game near his Oregon hometown. The home team was having a disastrous day, and every time they moved upfield, their drives were cut short by fumbles. Finally, in frustration, a guy a couple of rows ahead of Pesky stood up and roared, "Give the ball to Johnny Pesky. *He'll* hold onto it." It had been thirty-seven years since that disappointed six-year-old clicked off his radio—time enough for Nazi war criminals to have served out their sentences and be released—but when the alleged adult in the Yankee press box heard this story, he felt not just amusement but a vengeful delight. This feeling, though hardly to my credit, reflects the fact that the game itself permits, and even encourages, two conflicting ways of watching it.

The first is partisan, passionate, sometimes vindictive, and often as silly as George Steinbrenner's apology "to the people of New York" after the Yankees lost the 1981 World Series (or, for that matter, as my reaction to the Johnny Pesky story). The other, which savors the game as a graceful spectacle rather than a life-and-death struggle, is as generous as the vast green spaces of the outfield. The two work in tandem, the tension between them written inning by inning on the scoreboard, and the second is not necessarily "better" than the first. The sudden, crazy, adrenalized rush that etches an event forever in the memory—and that finally justifies the very notion of "spectator sports"—depends for its existence on partisanship. Without the emotional wager one makes in becoming a fan, even temporarily, there is little difference between watching baseball and watching Australian Rules football on ESPN—and none between a Mariners-Indians game in April and the September Baltimore-Yankees series.

Yet the palpable difference exists, for the players as well as for the fans; a game mediocre in all other respects can be genuinely thrilling when its outcome rewards a season of effort, a lifetime of rooting. Nevertheless, for fans, the aesthetic of partisanship is marred—fatally, I think—by its unstated presumption that the game is easy. That's why fans will boo their erstwhile heroes not just for lack of

< 141 >

effort but for failures in achievement. Tilted always toward blame, the presumption pinches praise.

Consider, for instance, Scott McGregor on the mound during the series' opening game. After his stop, his right knee rises, and his glove doesn't so much come up as pull back behind his leg, then behind his body. Only then, hidden from the batter, his left hand emerges from its shelter and whips around toward the plate. He throws at about three-quarters, rather than over the top, and left-handed batters don't get much of a look at the ball until it is almost on them, flickering away toward the outside corner of the plate. A right-hander has a fraction of a second longer to pick up the spin before committing himself, but left-handers have to decide early, and McGregor can make them look very foolish indeed.

In the fourth inning of that game, Nettles led off, and with a 1–1 count flailed at a fastball so high that Dempsey had to come up out of his squat to glove it. The next pitch, also up around Nettles's eyes, broke about a foot outside the plate and fooled him completely. Strike three, swinging, and to a scattering of boos Nettles sat.

It was, as it happened, another eye-high McGregor pitch that Nettles drove into the stands for the game-winning home run four innings later, and the fans who'd booed his strikeout no doubt contributed to the roar of approval that followed the homer. But because they'd earlier failed to appreciate just how hard it is for a left-hander to hit McGregor *at all,* their cheers were cheapened.

On the other hand, one recalls the story of the husband and wife who were seated in lawn chairs, sipping martinis and watching the stream at the edge of their backyard, when a bear came out of the woods and began to grapple with the man. His wife, watching the struggle, swirled her glass and said, "Go it, husband. . . . Go it, bear." Neutrality is sometimes out of place, and though a baseball game can indeed be a work of art, it ain't a chamber concert.

But at least for the past decade, the Mets might as well have been playing string quartets from the All-Star break on. And since it simply hasn't mattered to anyone much over the age of twelve whether they won or lost, it's been easy for fans at Shea to practice the aesthetic of neutrality. Indeed, it's been more than easy, it's been necessary; and since the pleasures of this aesthetic are in some crucial sense incom-

< 142 >

plete, the crowds at Shea have tended to be not only decorous but small.

It is, however, *possible* to enjoy both pleasures simultaneously—even at the Stadium. In a season's sampling of various locations, I found fans getting the best of both worlds at either extreme of the Stadium's rigidly enforced caste lines. Generosity and passion coexisted both in the most expensive—and often empty, though sold—season boxes and in the right-field bleachers. Those distant $1.50 seats are a wonderful place to watch a baseball game. They are about the only place in the Stadium—except for the playing field, of course—where black and Latin faces are likely to outnumber whites, and the prevailing mood out there is dope-drenched joy. The bleacher fans are surely partisan—they ride opposition right fielders unmercifully, and the cowbell-and-whistle brigade is at its most delirious during Yankee rallies—but they are also there for the spectacle, for the party.

Which spectacle is, I admit, often enhanced for them by the ubiquitous "Yankee joints" (a buck apiece, in pinstriped paper), that much encourage the virtue of patience. I don't want to give the impression that the bleachers look like an outtake from some Cheech and Chong movie, but a lot of people out there are, you know, "into" beauty—and capable of recognizing it even when it comes in the form of a rally-snuffing double play executed by the visiting team.

Except for those two parts of the Stadium, however, Yankee crowds seem almost universally dedicated to a bottom-line aesthetic: winning is what matters, and Gossage and Smalley *deserved* to be booed. Though this didn't make the Stadium fans pleasant company, they were not entirely to be blamed for their behavior, for they were aping the attitude that Steinbrenner—as sturdy a partisan as ever walked the streets unsupervised—had made respectable. An investment of one's heart is at least as meaningful as an investment of one's wallet, and these spiritual investors were merely providing a mass version of Steinbrenner's famous 1981 apology or his 1982 statements (after he'd let Reggie Jackson go to California) that Dave Winfield "wasn't a winner." Early in the owner's reign, Yankee players had had only one Steinbrenner to contend with; ten years into it, the Stadium was filled with thousands of them.

The original model Steinbrenner, it should be noted, was behaving

< 143 >

with uncharacteristic maturity at this point. He had, it's true, bad-mouthed Smalley and demanded videotapes so he could review the umpire's calls on Gossage's walk to Dempsey, but when he visited the Yankee clubhouse between games he threw no temper tantrums. Indeed, he went over, sat by Goose, and told him not to get down. There was an element of self-servingness here, to be sure—Steinbrenner was well aware of Gossage's disaffection and didn't want to lose him to free agency—but there might have been generosity as well. Yet it was too late for Steinbrenner's attempts at understanding to make any difference, and not simply for Gossage. Above his head, in the stands, the monster he'd created was already loose, and it would be years, if ever, before it was once again captured.

As the second game started, the fans were flat, acting almost as though the game were already lost. After all, the nightcap was the one game in the series the Yankees were "supposed" to lose—their lone right-handed starter, John Montefusco, going against Baltimore rookie Mike Boddicker—and even when the Yankees gave them some reasons to cheer, the fans responded guardedly. The tepid reaction was rational, perhaps, but only in the sense that neurotics' various strategies are. If one believes that love inevitably leads to betrayal, one withholds affection. Having spewed out their anger, the crowd had little left but fatalism; and when Willie Randolph was thrown out trying to steal in the Yankee first, the crowd's groan was dully resigned.

The book on Boddicker—who, as he demonstrated in the playoffs and the World Series, is one heckuva pitcher—is that you have to get to him early. He has such impeccable control, such an ability to be always on the black, that it takes umpires an inning or two to start believing in him and giving him the calls. In the first, the Yankees certainly had their opportunities. In addition to Randolph's single, they had a hustled infield hit from Winfield, a gift base when Boddicker threw away a pickoff throw, and a solid double from Nettles. All this activity, however, netted them only one run. Whether Altobelli read Martin's mind or his signs is still unknown, but he called for a pitchout as Randolph was stealing, and the call both nullified Randolph's good jump and cost the Yankees their chance to get to Boddicker early.

After that first inning, they showed no signs of getting him at all.

< 144 >

From then until there were only two outs remaining in the ninth, just one Yankee got as far as second base, and Smalley's one-out double in the fifth was wasted as Moreno grounded out and Randolph went down swinging.

Montefusco, however, was being unexpectedly tough on the Orioles. Through the first five innings, he allowed only three hits, giving up a run in the fourth when Singleton followed Lowenstein's two-out double with an r.b.i. single to right. But during the fifth, Montefusco began to be troubled by a recurring blister on his thumb, and the Baltimore sixth started with Rudy May on the mound for only his second appearance since mid-June. Though Martin had other pitchers available, the switch to a left-hander seemed worth the risk, as the predictable Altobelli would switch to his right-handed platoon. May began, however, with four straight balls to Dan Ford, who was pinch-hitting for Dwyer, then threw a fifth to Ripkin. His first pitch over the plate was a fastball up, and Ripkin lined a double to right, moving Ford to third.

This time, Martin chose not to walk Murray, and with the infield in May got him to ground out unassisted to Griffey, and the runners didn't advance. As predicted, Altobelli brought Roenicke up as a pinch hitter for Lowenstein, and Martin countered by bringing right-handed George Frazier in from the bullpen. Here, the temptation to call for an intentional walk must have been greater, for now a double-play could end the inning and keep Baltimore from scoring. Since Roenicke was followed in the batting order by Ken Singleton, whose speed had long since deserted him, that seemed the logical play. But Singleton was a switch-hitter, and Roenicke was at a comparative disadvantage against Frazier, so Martin chose to have the right-hander pitch to him.

Almost as a side effect of this decision, Martin had to play his infield in for the second batter in a row. This is always a choice a manager hates to make, for balls that would be playable at normal depth can skip through a semicircle of drawn-in infielders. But with the comparatively speedy Ford at third and only one out, the Yankees had no other choice. Frazier's first pitch jammed Roenicke, who swung defensively and flared a blooper to the right side of second base. Randolph turned and raced for the ball, but it fell inches beyond his outstretched glove; the extra ten feet he'd had to travel had cost the

< 145 >

Yankees a run. Only one run, however, for until the very last second, it had appeared that Randolph might be able to chase the ball down, and the runners had held their bases until the ball dropped.

With runners on first and third, and still only one out, Frazier struck out Singleton, and when he got Joe Nolan to pop a fly to short center, it appeared the Yankees would get out of the inning trailing by only a run. But Moreno, who'd sprinted to the ball in plenty of time, let it pop in and out of his glove. Ripkin scored from third, and Nolan, who'd never slowed down, reached second for a two-base error. Roenicke, however, had been so sure the ball would be caught that he'd started to jog and had failed to score. He died there when Frazier got a routine fly to Winfield to end the inning.

That was the end of the scoring. The Yankees outhit the Orioles, but hadn't taken advantage of the few opportunities given them; the O's had combined one solid hit with a walk, a Texas Leaguer, and an error to sweep the doubleheader.

Though the games were rife with opportunities for second-guessing, the closest anyone in the locker room came to challenging Martin was a polite question about whether Rawley had been tired when Martin pulled him during the first game. To his credit, Martin said, "No. He could've gone for a little more. He just made some bad pitches sometimes, and got himself in trouble a lot with walks, but he wasn't tired." After allowing himself the wistful comment that "the second game might've been different if we'd won the first," he focused on the future: "Tomorrow's gonna be the real challenge for us. Two tough losses tonight and then a day game . . . our pitching's gotta do it for us. Righetti's gotta pitch us a good ballgame."

Outside the manager's office, Gossage indulged in a little second-guessing of himself. Talking about the sequence of fastballs to Nolan, he said, "I wanted to throw a slider in there a couple of times, but Butch just kept putting fastballs down and I kept throwing it." He added that there had been no way for him to shake Wynegar off, "because, shit, if I do that, everyone in the park knows I'm gonna throw the slider."

There was probably some truth to the latter remark, but it's equally true that when Gossage was on the mound he didn't do a whole lot of analyzing. He preferred to be a throwing machine and let his catchers do the thinking for him. Perhaps more than any other Yan-

< 146 >

kee pitcher, then, his success was tied with how well the catcher set his rhythms, and during the year, Cerone had often been critical of the way Wynegar handled Gossage. I'd tended to dismiss Cerone's arguments as sour grapes from a guy who'd lost his starting job—a position also taken by bullpen coach Jeff Torborg—but the season's statistics actually bear Cerone out.

GOSSAGE PERFORMANCE					
Catcher	appearances	saves	wins	losses	no-decisions
Cerone	21	14	3	1	3
Wynegar	32	6	10	4	12

To understand the magnitude of the difference these figures reveal, one has to remember how Martin generally used Gossage. With only one or two exceptions (the first Baltimore game being an example), Gossage didn't come in when the Yankees were tied or behind. He came in during save situations, to protect an existing lead. Thus for Gossage, a "win" represents at least a partial failure; it means he let the other team tie or get ahead, thus becoming the pitcher of record, and that the Yankee batters had bailed him out. Similarly, the no-decision category reflects a failure, generally, that Gossage let runners on base score, but that the runs—and the loss—were charged to the man he'd relieved. Given that, the disparity between Gossage's performance with the two different catchers is enormous. Wynegar caught Gossage 50 percent more than Cerone did, but Cerone was the catcher in 70 percent of Gossage's saves (Espino caught two). To put it another way, when Cerone was catching, Gossage had a two-out-of-three chance at picking up a save; with Wynegar, his chances were less than one in five.

Wynegar had also been the catcher for four of the five home runs hit off Gossage during the season, and one would have imagined that Gossage, if no one else, would have been aware that there was some sort of problem. But if so, he never mentioned it to Martin or any of the coaches, and the closest he came to a complaint all year was that mild second-guess after having been shelled in the biggest game of the season. Beyond that, his only reaction was, "What can I say? I been

< 147 >

the hero, and I been the goat. Been both a lot of times this year, and a lot of times in my career. Tonight I was the goat for sure, but we're not out of it yet. I'll get my chance to be the hero."

This was, of course, the only reaction a short reliever *could* have and stay sane, and it was a far cry from the funk that had settled on Smalley. Hearing that Steinbrenner had been upstairs criticizing him, Smalley said, "Listen, he's just one out of fifty-six thousand. But whether you guys know this or whether George knows this doesn't matter to me: 'I don't give a fuck.' There isn't anybody in this clubhouse who works harder at being good at this game than I do, and I can look at myself in the mirror and say I gave it my best shot. I made some good plays, and I threw a ball away.

"I caught that ball, had everything under control, and I threw it right over Griffey's head. I don't know why the fuck that happened. The ball didn't slip out of my hands, and I wasn't nervous about playing in a big series, but I threw the ball away. You can blame me, you can blame God, you can blame Darwin, genes, wherever you think we get our ability. . . . I just threw the ball away.

"And the problem I have is not that it happened but that it's happened to me so much this year. Last year I made the fewest errors of any shortstop in the league, and you could count on one hand the number of errors I made after the seventh inning when my team had the lead. The worst part about this season is not being able to figure out *why*. I mean, shit, I've made so many errors in my life that it usually doesn't bother me, but *these* errors really do. I know when I've failed because I've been afraid of failing. I've done that. But I couldn't have felt more comfortable or more aggressive at shortstop than I felt tonight—and I *still* threw the ball away."

Smalley, who remained engaged in the thankless task of analyzing his own failures long after the reporters had left, closed out the evening in Martin's office, receiving during those early-morning hours whatever comfort the manager had to give. Interestingly, during his litany of things that might have been the cause but weren't, Smalley didn't once mention his illness. He'd been so dizzy that there had been some doubt whether he'd be able to play in the series at all, and in fact when he turned up at the ballpark the next day, he was too sick to play.

< 148 >

There were other problems as well: Wynegar was still unable to bat righty, Nettles needed a rest and even under the best conditions, he'd always had trouble against Oriole left-hander Mike Flanagan, and Martin didn't want to risk giving Dayett his first major league start in a big game. As a result, the bottom part of the line-up was punchless, and before the game Martin was reduced to black humor. "Look at this lineup," he said. "If we win today, it'll be a miracle. Righetti'll have to pitch another no-hitter. Once you get past Oscar, who's in there because Mattingly's not swinging the bat well, it's Campy, Cerone, Milbourne, and Moreno—'Bullets' Moreno," he added in a reference to his new center fielder's .222 average. "Christ, it makes *me* want to be a pitcher."

The hot afternoon did not, however, start off smoothly for Flanagan. Willie Randolph led off with a line double to left, and Griffey followed with a bullet single to center, giving the Yankees runners on first and third with no out, and Winfield, Baylor, and Gamble coming to the plate.

Except that's not the way it happened. Randolph and Griffey got the hits, all right, but Zimmer—in a truly inexplicable move—waved Randolph home from third. It wasn't even close; Shelby's throw got him by five feet. I say "inexplicable" because Zimmer's own postgame explanation—"I had a horseshit day"—seems somehow incomplete. Zimmer had been around long enough to know that Altobelli wasn't about to move his infield in that early in the game—so Randolph could have scored from third on a soft grounder as well as a reasonably deep fly. One has to figure that Winfield and Baylor between them could have produced one or the other. Under those circumstances, the run that the Yankees *might* have gained from Randolph's scoring wasn't worth the disastrous effect on a potentially very big inning if he'd been caught. So why did Zimmer do it?

There are a couple of possible explanations: he might have been misled by Shelby's weak throw toward the plate in the second game of the series, or he might have considered that with that day's Yankee lineup the team should go for every run it could. But these don't wash. The Yankee scouting reports credit Shelby with an adequate arm, and, of course, it wasn't the soft spot of the lineup coming to the plate, but the number three, four, and five hitters. Instead, it seems far more

< 149 >

likely that Zimmer's was a panic move, an unconscious response to the Yankees' desperate need to salvage a split if they weren't to drop out of the pennant race entirely.

In the next inning, however, it became clear that any thoughts about squeezing out a run here and a run there and relying on Righetti to hold the Orioles down were badly mistaken. Facing nine men without retiring the side, Righetti gave up six hits and a walk before leaving for Roger Erickson with the score 5–0, Orioles, and Baltimore runners at first and third. Oddly, however, the game wasn't quite yet over, for Erickson ended the inning by striking out Eddie Murray, and for the rest of the game held the O's to three hits and no runs. Inevitably, his performance raised the question of where he'd been all year, especially during the pre-Montefusco games when the Yankees' right-handed pitchers had qualified for federal disaster aid. He'd been at Columbus—not pitching particularly well, it's true (though he said that was because he was bored and had already proved he could pitch Triple-A baseball)—and hadn't been called up because he was being punished for his early-season refusal to return meekly to the minors. Hearing that the front office had insisted he was still in the Yankees' future, he'd said, "I don't even want to be in their present."

Through the next couple of innings, Flanagan held the Yankees hitless, but in the fourth the Yankees threatened again. Griffey led off with a sharp single to left, and took second when Rich Dauer was barely able to make a diving stab of Winfield's behind-the-runner grounder. Baylor then drove a sharply lined single to center, and— in a virtual replay of the first-inning films—Zimmer once again sent a runner home from third, and Shelby once again threw him out by a generous margin. If the first inning play had been inexplicable, this one—with the Yankees down 5–0 and in dire need of a big inning— was inexcusable.

The Yankees, however, didn't quit, picking up a run in the seventh, when Baylor doubled to right and Cerone hit a two-out single to center, and two in the ninth, when Winfield drew a leadoff walk and trotted home after Baylor's booming home run into the left-field stands. Flanagan got the first out on Gamble's grounder, but when he gave up a pinch-hit single to Balboni, he was gone, and Altobelli brought in Tippy Martinez to close the game out. Cerone hit Martinez's first pitch deep, but into the playable reaches of Death Valley,

< 150 >

and the Yankees were down to their final out. With Milbourne due at the plate, a pinch hitter was an inevitability, but when Martin—hesitant to bring Dayett up in such a crucial situation—signaled to Nettles, the Yankee captain said he'd always had trouble with Martinez. In angry desperation, Martin turned to the ailing Smalley, who grounded into a force play that effectively ended the New York pennant race.

After the game, the Yankees seemed resigned to their situation, and Nettles spoke for most of them when he said, "I'd be surprised if the Orioles didn't win. The way they're playing right now, I can't see them going into any kind of nose dive. There's no question they outplayed us in this series," he added, then singled out Joe Altobelli for praise, "You've gotta say something for the managing over there; Joe did a helluva job. He didn't have Palmer for a couple of months, didn't have Flanagan for a couple of months, and I think Dennis [Martinez] was one-and-ten for a while.

"But they didn't panic. They got Boddicker up from the minors; and he's been real good for them, and the trade they made for Cruz, though I didn't think it was the greatest thing they've ever done, worked out real well. Plus," he added, in what can only be construed as criticism of Martin, "there's a calmness and stability over there. They know when they're gonna be in the lineup, know what's gonna happen from day to day."

Nettles was still smarting from Martin's reaction to his backing away from the ninth-inning pinch-hitting, but the Baltimore platooning system Altobelli had inherited from Weaver unquestionably provided the Oriole players with the kind of security Martin's Yankees lacked. Yet it's a long way from certain that such a system would have worked in New York. To begin with, Altobelli had not only taken over an established pattern of platooning, he'd taken over an established ball club. The '82 Orioles had finished sixteen games over .500 and only a game out of first; the '82 Yankees, four games below .500, had been only a game out of last. Altobelli had been hired to continue, Martin to innovate.

Still, he'd surprised his employers before. He *could* have platooned, pairing Gamble with Baylor, Piniella with Kemp, and Cerone with Wynegar. Gamble and Piniella, long used to being platoon players in the Baltimore mode, would have had no problem, and Cerone would

< 151 >

surely have been happier platooned than demoted. In fact, Martin had done some platooning with his catchers early in the season, but Steinbrenner had effectively ordered that Wynegar be the full-time starter during his April meeting with Martin in Texas. And long before he'd hired Martin—when he was wooing Kemp and Baylor to New York as free agents—Steinbrenner had promised them starting slots. He'd never been averse to breaking his promises when situations changed—he did not, for instance, second-guess when Martin began playing Mattingly over the slumping Kemp—but Steinbrenner had spent millions of dollars to bring those two players to the Yankees, and it's difficult to believe he would have sat back and watched them playing only part-time in the early season. Martin, reclusive and aloof, was surely not the type of manager one would choose to persuade such players to accept part-time status, but no 1983 Yankee manager would have had a chance to undertake such a process.

Further, of course, there's no guarantee that platooning would have produced results any better than Martin's ad hoc approach. Both Kemp and Baylor had been regulars throughout their careers, and no matter what their frames of mind, many players find the shifting rhythm of part-time play a difficult adjustment. Kemp's season was admittedly disappointing, and he might have had better results if he'd faced right-handers exclusively, but Baylor, who played more games than any Yankee except Winfield, wound up hitting over .300 for the first time in his professional career. Calm and stability may well be valuable to a team, but no club in baseball was more cantankerous and ornery than the 1983 Phillies, and it was they, not the compliant Dodgers, who represented their league in the World Series.

< 152 >

11

Scapegoats

The day after the crucial Baltimore series limped to its close, as the Yankees prepared to begin a three-game series with the Brewers, Steinbrenner came into the clubhouse to address a pregame meeting. Citing Berra's famous "It's not over till it's over," he urged the team to keep trying, saying he certainly didn't want to finish third or fourth —that if they couldn't win, they should at least be second: "If we're gonna go down, let's go down proud." He concluded by adding— perhaps fearful that appeals to pride might not be fully persuasive— that anyone who didn't hustle was going to find his ass in trouble.

As Steinbrenner performances go, this one—according to a player who'd endured many—was on the muted side. But there are persuasive indications that Steinbrenner's heart wasn't in it, for he almost instantly began acting as though he believed the season was over. Typically, this involved the search for scapegoats, and before the week was out he had nominated three—or, perhaps, three-and-a-half.

Dave Winfield was his first candidate, and the echoes of Steinbrenner's appeals to Yankee glory had barely died away when the owner began telling reporters, "not for attribution," that Winfield hadn't done his job in the season's big series. Winfield's overall statistics might have looked good, said the owner, but he was batting only .210

< 153 >

against Milwaukee and .184 versus Baltimore, and in the eleven games against the O's Winfield had produced only two r.b.i.'s. He was a good player, sure, but you couldn't count on him in September.

When these comments were relayed to him, Winfield's initial response was short and telling. "Without me," he said, "there wouldn't *be* any big games in September." This was by and large true, and there were other problems with the charge as well. Prior to the Baltimore series, the Yankees' most important confrontation of the season had come in Detroit, as they faced a divisional rival in the midst of the pine-tar slump. Over the four-game stretch, Winfield had collected seven hits in fifteen at bats, including three doubles and three home runs; he'd also scored five runs and driven in seven, a performance hardly that of someone who choked in big games. He was, however, undeniably a streak hitter, and like most streak hitters capable of looking truly terrible when a big series coincided with one of his fallow periods. It had happened to Winfield during the 1981 World Series, when he went 1-for-22. But it also happened on and off to Baltimore's Eddie Murray during this season—most notably during the championship series and the first four World Series games. Murray, as a matter of fact, had gone 3-for-15 in the series against the Yankees, without even a single r.b.i., but his failure to produce had gone relatively unremarked because the Orioles had done well.

As expected, Winfield soon emerged from his mini-slump; after a day off and a slow beginning, he went 3-for-4 in the final Milwaukee game, then couldn't have been hotter during the next series. In three games against Cleveland, away, Winfield was 10-for-15, with three home runs and seven r.b.i.'s. Yet, as Winfield later pointed out, the Yankees lost two of those three games and had only split in Detroit. It is difficult even to imagine a player being more productive than Winfield during those seven games, but no one player can do enough for his team to win—or lose—in major league baseball.

The most interesting question about Steinbrenner's charges, however, involved not their demonstrable obtuseness but the fact that he made them at all. The Yankees weren't even close to being mathematically eliminated from the division race, and though a fatal Baltimore slump was unlikely it was hardly impossible. Why attack Winfield *now?*

At the time, the only explanation seemed to be that Steinbrenner

< 154 >

wasn't entirely of sound mind. Strong as the urge might have been, to avoid taking any blame on himself for the Yankees' disappointing showing, Steinbrenner's efforts to blame Winfield seemed somewhere between ludicrous and loony.

But there was, it developed, an explanation admitting at least a tincture of rationality, which Winfield himself revealed in Baltimore, shortly before the season's final game. "I've been having some trouble with George, again," he said. "With the foundation, same as last time. I don't want this printed yet, because we're still negotiating, but there really shouldn't *need* to be a negotiation. The man made a commitment, and he's not honoring it."

That commitment, a written agreement entered into at the time Winfield signed with the Yankees, called for payments of $300,000 a year to the David M. Winfield Foundation, a tax-exempt charity of which Winfield was the founder and hands-on director. Steinbrenner had reneged on this payment once before, and after Winfield had brought suit the parties reached an out-of-court settlement.

Shortly after the '83 season, Winfield went public with his dissatisfaction, suing Steinbrenner for a second time. During their first confrontation in 1981, Steinbrenner had freely admitted not making the payments but had claimed it was because the foundation was improperly registered and its board overloaded with family members. The implication of these statements was that Winfield was milking his foundation and that only Steinbrenner's alertness was preventing some sort of sophisticated ripoff.

No matter what the situation may have been earlier, however, the state attorney general's office in New Jersey, where the foundation keeps its offices, confirmed that it was both properly registered and up-to-date with its filings and that the composition of its board was "in no significant way exceptional."

Apparently lacking any legal justification for his delay in payments to the foundation, Steinbrenner might have anticipated that Winfield would once again be forced to take him to court. In that case, his apparently irrational attacks on Winfield's performance might have been designed to give the public the impression that the outfielder hadn't even been earning his salary, much less any additional contributions to his foundation. This sort of preemptive media strike in what Steinbrenner had reason to believe would become a public battle

< 155 >

was in poor taste at best—especially while Winfield was keeping silent during negotiations—but it at least admits a method to the Yankee owner's malice.

Winfield, however, was only the first in a player lineup of Steinbrenner's designated scapegoats; Roy Smalley was next. Steinbrenner's criticisms of Smalley immediately after he'd made two key errors in the Baltimore series lacked the economic explanation of his attack on Winfield, but they could be partly excused as an emotional reaction to a difficult loss. The owner's next move, however, was calculated. While the team was in Cleveland, he leaked word that Andre Robertson would be facing a "substantial" fine—probably $5,000, more than 10 percent of his salary—for having broken curfew the night of his auto accident. Steinbrenner offered a conditional rationale for a fine this size: it was justified, "If as some people have said," the loss of Robertson cost the Yankees a pennant and, hence, about a million dollars in postseason receipts. But by planning to levy it, Steinbrenner announced that he, for once, accepted the condition as true.

The players were not amused, and their gallows humor—"At that rate," said Nettles, "Thurman's lucky he killed himself"—was bitter. Many of them had thought at the time that Robertson had done something foolish, but none of the players—then, or at any time during the season—had been *angry*. They'd been, and remained, sorry for him, especially because, as the Yankee front office gradually revealed word of how serious his injury actually was, the players realized that Robertson's career might be over. If Steinbrenner was right, Robertson had taken some $50,000 away from each of them, but there wasn't the slightest evidence that any of the players were at all resentful. That's not because baseball players are indifferent to money—whether examining the phone calls listed on their hotel bills or negotiating multimillion-dollar contracts, they care—but because they appreciate how lucky they are to be playing a game for a living. Knowing that Robertson might never again share that joy had touched them, reminded them of their own vulnerability and the fragile nature of their pleasures, and they were universally disgusted by Steinbrenner's crassness.

Moreover, as Winfield said in his capacity as player representative, such a fine would almost certainly be uncollectable. The Yankees had never enforced a home curfew (even the announced road curfew was

< 156 >

generally ignored), and even if the team had had a policy of sending coaches all over the New York suburbs to conduct bed checks, Martin would effectively have exempted the rookie from such a curfew when he told Robertson he was going to have the next day off. "He'd been having some trouble at the plate," Martin recalled, "and was starting to press, so I told him I was going to rest him for a couple of days."

Given the patent ineffectualness of the fine as a remedy for any of Steinbrenner's various woes, it seemed a gratuitous gesture whose sole discernible purpose was to humiliate Smalley by announcing to all the world that if he hadn't been playing shortstop, the Yankees would have won the pennant.

For Smalley, this was the final insult in a troubled season—in fact, a troubled Yankee career. He'd come to the club from Minnesota, a week into the 1982 season, in a much-second-guessed trade that had cost the Yankees reliever Ron Davis. Davis, with Gossage, had provided the Yankees with a nearly unstoppable bullpen combination during the 1981 season, and the decision to get rid of him—for anyone —had been unpopular.

The decision to trade him for a shortstop seemed particularly strange. In Bucky Dent, the Yankees already had one of the league's premier defensive shortstops. Dent was popular not only with the fans —he'd been a best-selling poster boy ever since his home run in the 1978 playoff—but also with those most rigorous judges of fielding performance, the Yankee pitchers, who were not at all eager to see him replaced.

At that time, many of the Yankee players felt that Smalley wasn't being brought over primarily to play short but to replace Nettles at third when the Yankee captain finally yielded to age. During the 1982 season, there were indications that the inevitable was indeed happening to Nettles—though he continued to field strongly, his .232 batting average was his lowest since his rookie season in 1969—and Smalley divided his playing time between short (89 games) and third (53 games).

But things had changed by the start of the '83 season. Dent was gone, and more importantly, Martin was among the handful of professional observers who thought Nettles could still be a productive everyday player. In this, at least, Martin was right; after a horrendously slow start which saw Steinbrenner calling for him to be benched,

< 157 >

Nettles wound up raising his batting average by thirty-two points and his r.b.i.'s from fifty-five to seventy-five, third on the club. Martin also tagged Smalley as his starting shortstop, and in this, Steinbrenner was sure the manager was wrong. Steinbrenner wanted Andre Robertson to play short and Smalley to play third; unable to budge Martin on Nettles, he was insistent that Robertson be given a shot as shortstop. "At that time," said a person close to Steinbrenner, "George was looking at Nettles's numbers and was sure that even Billy was going to have to start sitting him down. When that happened, Smalley would get his playing time, but at third."

In the event, however, Nettles' bat recovered its quickness and Robertson—about whose fielding abilities there had never been any question—was hitting the ball unexpectedly well. There was, it appeared, no room for Smalley. He filled in occasionally for Nettles at third, for Griffey at first, and played short only when Randolph's injuries moved Robertson to second. At thirty, in what should theoretically have been the prime of his career, he was becoming a part-time ballplayer.

And, predictably, an unhappy one. By mid-July, as he sat in the dugout one day watching the rainstorm that had washed out batting practice before a game with Texas, Smalley was saying, "I'm a good player, and I deserve to play every day. If not here, then somewhere else." He said this without at all taking away from Robertson's skills —"I know I can't play short the way the kid does, not too many people can"—but added, "I think I'm still an asset at shortstop. I don't have the kid's range, but I play the hitters well, and when the ball's hit to me, I catch it. I can also play third," he added. "Last year I played fifty-three games there, and I was starting to learn that position, to feel comfortable out there."

Was he comfortable watching Robertson play short and waiting for Nettles to retire? "*This* year, for the rest of this season, I am. I can understand the situation, but if Puff comes back next year and is getting to play, I could ill-afford another season. It's just not good not to play—not psychologically, not physically. Physically, your skills atrophy, and psychologically, if you're playing every day, an individual ball you don't reach or hit you don't get, you can shrug off and say you're gonna get the next one. And if you *feel* like you're gonna get the next one, you probably will. Baseball's a grind-it-out type of

< 158 >

existence, and it really rewards consistency. But when you're playing only occasionally, it's much harder to get those missed opportunities out of your head—and there are likely to be more of them because of the physical side.

"Sure, when you're playing every day and you're not swinging the bat well, you can go from oh-for-four to oh-for-twenty pretty quick, but your streakiness will work the other way for you, too. Playing part-time, you may not get down in the numbers so quick, but getting back up is almost impossible. Even a platoon player knows when he's gonna be playing and when he's not, so with a little adjustment of his expectations and rhythms, he can become what amounts in his head to an everyday player. But if you come out to the park never knowing if you're gonna be playing, where you're gonna be playing, where you're gonna be batting if you *are* playing, it inevitably hurts your ability to perform up to your capabilities."

There is, I think, some evidence that Smalley was right, but the central question raised by Steinbrenner's fining Robertson wasn't whether Smalley had played up to his capabilities but whether his playing in place of Robertson had cost the Yankees the pennant. Here, the evidence seems overwhelmingly against Steinbrenner: the Yankees were by far a prettier team with Robertson at short, but all in all they were a better team with Smalley. The gap between the two on the field was certainly real, as even Smalley admitted, but not as important as the differences between them at the plate.

Though Robertson certainly started out more strongly than anyone had expected as a batter—on June 17, he was hitting .265—he tailed off disastrously, and by the time he was finally "rested"—and injured—his average had fallen to .248. This in itself might have been tolerable, for a team with the Yankees' power could at least theoretically afford to carry a slick-fielding shortstop who wasn't a big hitter, but the low batting average was the least of Robertson's troubles as a hitter. In his 322 at bats, he had struck out 54 times and walked only 8. This strikeout to at bat ratio was the worst among Yankees who had 300 or more at bats, and the 1:6 figure wasn't at all counterbalanced by home run power. Big-swinging power hitters might be able to get away with such a figure (though in fact, the Yankees' two leading home run hitters, Winfield and Baylor, had ratios of 1:8 and 1:10), but Robertson was by force of circumstance a contact hitter,

< 159 >

and to be successful his ratio should at least have approached Willie Randolph's 1:13.

Perhaps because of his tendency to swing at bad pitches, Robertson's failure to help the Yankees at the plate was most dramatically reflected in his failure to draw bases on balls. Randolph, with his 32 strikeouts, had 53 walks (another indication why he was one of the game's premier leadoff hitters), and even a notorious bad-ball hitter like Nettles, who often chased—and hit—high pitches, balanced his 65 strikeouts with 51 walks. Smalley, who struck out 68 times, piled up 58 walks, which translated into 50 more times on base than Robertson.

The failure to get on base, as well as the failure to move runners around by making contact with the ball, made Robertson a singularly unproductive batter. According to my noncomputerized use of the Bill James formula, Robertson produced only twenty-seven runs for the Yankees, compared to Smalley's seventy-five—and the gap actually widens when one calculates runs per game by figuring in the outs created. As a more conventional way of measuring the gap, we can look at the two standard productivity measures for each player: Smalley, with 62 r.b.i.'s and 70 runs scored in 130 games, contributed 1.02 runs per game; Robertson, with 22 r.b.i.'s and 37 runs scored in 98 games, was responsible for .59. In a projected season in which one or the other played full time (150 games), Smalley would have contributed 153 runs, Robertson 85. The 68 run difference between the two is more than marginally significant. Over the entire season, the Yankees outscored their rivals by only 67 runs, and 42 of their 91 victories were by one or two-run margins.

That offensive difference must, however, be reduced by some figure to reflect Robertson's superior defensive skills. Here, the evidence is necessarily a little more subjective, but not entirely so. After Robertson's injury, virtually all the reporters who regularly covered the Yankees made a note of each ground-ball hit that got by Smalley but that would have been within Robertson's range. Such hits occurred, on a generous estimate, perhaps once every five games. Over the same projected 150-game season that saw an offensive gap of 68 runs, this translates into 30 extra hits for the Yankees' opponents. Over the actual season, every opponent's base hit equalled .485 runs, so those projected hits were worth 15 runs. Thus, over a full projected season,

< 160 >

the Yankees would have been 53 runs stronger with Smalley in the lineup than with Robertson.

Even if you tinker with the assumptions and say that Robertson would have prevented a hit every three games (something the evidence doesn't warrant, but never mind), there's still a difference of more than 40 runs, and at that, the difference is understated. Virtually all of the Smalley-hits a Robertson might have prevented were singles, and the .485 runs-per-hit figure includes doubles, triples, and home runs (on which neither fielder could have had much of an influence). If you do nothing more than deduct homers, the run-per-hit figure falls to .440.

Even allowing some subjective defensive benefits from Robertson (the Yankee pitchers unquestionably felt more confident with him out there, for instance), Steinbrenner's implied charge that Smalley was responsible for losing the pennant is ludicrous. To a degree, Smalley knew this, and felt that the criticism from the owner and from the fans was unjust, but he was also acutely aware that his fielding had cost the team some games: he might not have been nearly as bad as Steinbrenner apparently thought he was, but neither was he as good as he believed he should have been.

All ballplayers, of course, believe they should approach perfection; an ego of that sort is necessary to most individual professional efforts —it's what enables dancers to weather auditions, novelists to brave rejection slips. Smalley's drive for achievement may have been slightly more refined than some of the other players—as the son of a professional ballplayer, he bore some additional psychological burdens— but no major leaguer is likely to blame his failures on a lack of talent (nor, in general, should he; lack of talent shows up in the minors). Looking around for the source of his disappointing season, Smalley settled on the manager. "I've played three positions this year," he said in a late-season interview, "and maybe two-thirds of the games. I've also batted just about everywhere in the lineup—a few times in the heavy r.b.i. positions, a lot at seventh or eighth, or even ninth, and I even led off once or twice.

"I started out thinking, 'What's the difference? If you're a professional you ought to be able to handle it.' I found to my discredit that I didn't handle it very well, that I didn't play as well in *any* position as I would have in one.

< 161 >

"But I don't think that was true just of me. I failed, by my standards, but it wasn't what I'd call a personal failure, because what I found was that consistency *is* important. Baseball," he paused and looked for the right words, "is an endeavor of familiarity. Over a hundred and sixty-two games of human performance in a variable and dynamic environment, you're going to have days that'll just thrill you to death and days that are so horrible you can hardly stand to think about them. In that kind of circumstance, you need to be able to go back to your hotel room—or home to your wife and kids, ideally— saying, 'I'm coming out to do the same thing tomorrow.'

"That's not a quirk in my nature; it's in the nature of the game, and I think it would be true with any baseball player on any baseball team. But," he added, "it's especially important on this team. The Yankees are different from most organizations. You guys are here," he grinned, "in profusion, and everybody—the fans, the owner—has high expectations not only for individual performance but for team performance. Plus this year—well, you know how they say you'll see some one thing you've never seen before at every game?—this year, we've had it *all*. Pine tar, sea gulls, funny winds, suspensions, big games, important trades, coaches fired. . . . In this kind of situation, players *crave* stability."

With that need in mind, would he have managed the club differently? Used himself more consistently? "It would be easy to say, 'Yeah,' but I don't really know. The Yankee manager is supposed to *win,* and he's playing to a supercritical audience. Maybe in that circumstance—and with the multiplicity of talent on this team— there's no other way to have handled it. Put nine guys out there, your best nine, and suppose one of them is slumping real bad. Look at what's there just waiting on the bench. That might be too much of a temptation for any manager."

In the wake of the Baltimore debacle, some sort of second-guessing the manager was inevitable; what was unusual about Smalley's— given the blame he'd been absorbing—was it's tolerance. In searching for adjectives to describe Steinbrenner's however, you'd work through several hundred before coming to "tolerant." Even before the Yankees had completed the final three games of their homestand, the rumblings from upstairs began to be reflected in the media.

Two days after Baltimore left town, the *Daily News* back page

< 162 >

nominated Nettles as the 1984 Yankee manager. Bill Madden's column pointed out, correctly, that Nettles had a wide and sophisticated knowledge of the game, but what was most striking about his nomination was that Madden linked it directly to Gossage's return. In brief, the contention was that Gossage simply couldn't turn down a Yankee offer if his friend Nettles, as manager, asked him to sign with the team. This was the first suggestion that Gossage's well-known desire to escape the Yankees, a desire expressed with gathering strength ever since Steinbrenner's "apology" after the 1981 Series, could be effectively countered by a new manager.

It was not the last. Two mornings later, as the team left for Cleveland, both the *News* and the *Times,* in a virtual replay of Martin's mid-June "firing," announced that he was in trouble. Because of the way he'd managed, they reported, the Yankees were wracked with dissension: Don Zimmer had resigned, effective at the end of the season, because of him; Gossage's agent had told the Yankees that the reliever would refuse to come back to the team if Martin stayed; ditto Dale Murray's; one nameless player had demanded an extra half-million a year to sign with the Yankees if Martin was manager; Floyd Bannister had refused to consider the Yankees off-season offer when he was a free agent because it looked as though Martin was going to be the manager; Griffey wanted a trade because Martin had yelled at his son; Martin had ruined Kemp; Torborg and Ellis didn't want to come back if Martin was going to be there.

If even half the charges were true, the indictment was devastating, and Martin, who'd cheerfully joked about the Nettles-for-manager story, reacted angrily. On the plane to Cleveland, he talked in turn to Zimmer, Ellis, and Torborg, and by the time he reached the stadium he was ready with a point-by-point refutation. "Griffey *was* mad that one time," he said, "He had trouble with the security guard, but he's not mad at me. Dale's not mad at me either; he's mad at himself. I haven't pitched him 'cause he's not doing the job for us. Goose and I are good friends, real good friends, and what it comes down to is this. The 'reliable source' is full of shit—trying to make me a scapegoat. I can't take the blame for somebody else—especially when somebody else *is* 'the reliable source.' All George has to do is pick up the phone and I'll walk away like a man, but I hate to be lied about.

"Murray Chass put it in the paper that I was the reason Zim quit

< 163 >

and that's full of shit. Zim went up and told George, 'It's not Billy Martin, but I'm not coming back next year.' It was for his own personal reasons. And Goose, Goose has been mad for three years, everybody knows that. But his agent hasn't talked to *anybody*. It's gonna be shown there's no foundation to all this stuff, no foundation at all, because the players will say it. Of course it won't do any good at all, because the accusations are out and people will believe them. It's piss-poor journalism is all.

"And it's part of a well-designed plot, with professional leaks to those two writers. I think it's a cheap shot, as cheap as they come— especially now, when we haven't lost the pennant yet. When George gave his speech to all the players, he said 'play your hardest right up to the end, and I'll really appreciate it.' Well they *have* been. They won three in a row against Milwaukee, and now the 'reliable source' is screwing them up. It's almost like he didn't *want* them to win because it might screw up his plans. These guys don't need that, not right now. But I suppose it had to happen now because these things always break when we're in Cleveland. I gotta hand it to that reliable source, boy, he sure knows his stuff."

"Listen," he said, calming down briefly, "I expect certain guys to be mad: Cerone for not playing, Kemp for being beaten out, and I expect any pitcher who's not pitching to complain. But if *I* was the owner or general manager, I'd tell those guys 'just do your job.' My job isn't to win a popularity poll with them. My job is 'you ain't hittin', so you ain't playin'.' I don't take anybody out of the lineup; they take themselves out.

"And I *don't* have to talk to a guy who's hittin' .240— and I don't need to 'communicate' with a guy who's hittin' .340 either. I might have something to say to a rookie, maybe, but I'm not gonna tell a veteran who's hittin' .240 that he's doin' great, 'cause he's not. But I don't knock him in the papers, either. You'll *never* see me with a bunch of statistics saying this player or that player didn't do a job in a big series. I don't believe in that kind of stuff.

"I didn't complain when we lost Mumphrey either. I didn't like to lose him. He'd started to swing the bat real good again, especially left-handed, and I don't like to make changes when the team is going good, and right then we were winning. But I just said 'no comment,' and that's *all* I said. On the record or off the record. The guys who

< 164 >

wrote the stories in the paper today were used by someone who's a master of 'off the record,' who knows how to use, how to manipulate.

"I'll tell you the thing that makes me maddest, though. It's that shit about Griffey's kid. I never even spoke to the kid that night. I just told Sal [the security guard outside the locker room] to tell the kids to be quiet after we lose. When we win, kids are welcome to come right into the clubhouse, but not after a loss. My son, Billy Joe, he wouldn't *dare* come into the clubhouse after we'd lost. It's not supposed to be a party when you lose. But before a game, or after a win, they're welcome. I have fuckin' *candy* in my office for kids. . . ."

As if on cue, Griffey, looking stricken, appeared at the office door. He turned to leave when he saw reporters present—he would come back later for a private conversation—but Martin stopped him. "Wait a second, Griff. I want you to tell these guys something. Did I ever yell at your kids? Are you mad at me 'cause I yelled at your kids?"

"No. I was upset at the time about the fact that Nick [Priorie, the clubhouse man] approached me and didn't ask me to talk to my kids, but started ordering me. That's why I was pissed off. There were other kids out there too, but he just walked up to me and said, 'Tell your kids to be quiet.' That's why I exploded."

As Griffey talked, it began to seem that this particular round of rumored comings and goings might be more different from the earlier "firing" than it had at first seemed. In June, there had been no question that Steinbrenner had believed what he'd alleged—that Martin had defied him by not holding an off-day workout in Milwaukee, that Martin had been more attentive to a woman traveling companion than to the Yankees during that series of games, that he'd lost control of himself and busted up the dugout porcelain with a bat in Cleveland, and that Martin had told the *Times* researcher to suck his cock. Though the facts in all those cases were not—and indeed are not—entirely clear, Steinbrenner's sincerity had been indisputable. This time around, it was very much in doubt.

According to the *Times,* for instance, "A parade of agents, including Rich Gossage's representative, have told Steinbrenner in recent weeks that their clients no longer want to play for Martin." Since later on in the story, Murray Chass, a careful reporter, noted that "Gossage declined to comment on his feelings, and calls to his agent, Jerry Kapstein, were not returned," only Steinbrenner could have been the

< 165 >

source for the original information. Once it had been published, however, Gossage was more than willing to comment, and dismissed the leak as "a lot of crap. Sure I wish I'd gotten to come in more often at the start of an inning, so if there's any shit to clean up it's my own, but if anyone says I said I wouldn't play for this manager—for *any* manager—that's a fuckin' lie. I was unhappy before Billy got here, and I've been unhappy while he was here. But I *never* told anyone to tell George I wouldn't come back if Billy was here. And I know nobody did tell him that or I would have known."

Zimmer was equally emphatic in his denials. The *Times* had followed the Gossage information with: "Furthermore, it was learned yesterday, Don Zimmer has submitted his resignation as the Yankees' third-base coach, and sources linked Zimmer's move to his displeasure with working under Martin." Asked to comment on it, Zimmer said, "I never said one word about Billy when I told George I was leaving, the name never was mentioned. And when Murray Chass called me up at home last night to talk about it, I told him, 'You can't print that story. It's not true.' I wouldn't even tell him I was resigning at all."

Chass had reported Zimmer's refusal to comment, and even noted that one source said that Zimmer, "in resigning, had not cited Martin as the reason. However," the story continued, "other sources among the Yankees have said for some time that the 52-year-old Zimmer . . . had been unhappy working under Martin."

This last was certainly true. Zimmer had been frustrated by Lee Walls's arrival, disappointed that he'd been essentially left out of the successor speculation in mid-June (he made no secret of the fact that he wanted to manage again, somewhere), and *did* find it hard to deal with Martin's temper and fits of distraction. But he was hardly part of a "Dump Billy" movement. Hard-bitten and sometimes irascible, Zimmer was more than capable of getting into a screaming confrontation whenever he thought the occasion demanded, but back-stabbing was emphatically not his style.

Chass didn't make the Cleveland trip, but Madden, whose story had added Torborg and Ellis to the list of Yankees who didn't want to come back if Martin remained, was there, and as reporters entered the clubhouse, Torborg pulled Madden aside for a conversation that

< 166 >

began, "What did you write *that* for? You didn't even *talk* to me. . . ."

What was going on here? Was all this just a desperate sort of backpedaling from people who hadn't liked to read about the consequences of their actions? Had there indeed been a concerted effort to send Steinbrenner a message?

Or, perhaps, had Steinbrenner been so eager to perceive a message that he found one where none was intended? I suspect the latter. There were unquestionably a lot of unhappy Yankees, but at least as long as the team had had a realistic shot at the pennant, even the most frustrated had generally managed to keep their anger in check. With the team driving for a championship, nobody wanted to rock the boat. And for many Yankees, the possibility of a pennant had seemed quite real right up until the Baltimore series. Rick Cerone, for instance, who felt that Martin had betrayed him by yielding to Steinbrenner's forceful desire to play Wynegar, had gone so far as to describe Martin as "gutless," but when offered the opportunity to go to San Diego, where he could have played regularly, Cerone refused to waive the no-trade clause in his contract. "Why," he asked, "should I leave a contender for a club that doesn't have a shot at the pennant?"

But that didn't mean he was happy playing in Wynegar's shadow. Kemp and Murray were unhappy as well—though, as Martin suggested, part of their anger was very likely directed at themselves. But even Smalley, who had in fact played well up to the Yankees' reasonable expectations for him, had his share of criticisms about the manager, and Oscar Gamble—another player forced from the lineup by circumstance rather than his own failures—could hardly wait to get to a ball club where he could play more regularly. Under these conditions, it would have been surprising if Steinbrenner *hadn't* heard at least indirect expressions of discontent from these players, especially when most had managed—for the good of the team—to suppress their frustrations for so long.

But to draw from these isolated incidents, as Steinbrenner apparently chose to do, a picture of a Yankee clubhouse seething with resentment and frustration was to distort the situation beyond recognition. On the day after the stories saying Steinbrenner was once again ready to fire Martin appeared, there was indeed some angry yelling

< 167 >

in the locker room—but it had to do with what channel would be on the clubhouse television. Faced with a choice of a big college football game, a stakes race, and a prizefight, the Yankees were far more visibly and vocally divided than they were about the identity of their manager. That Steinbrenner was so ready to see, and encourage, dissatisfaction with Martin has far less to do with what was actually happening with his team than with his own continuing inability to face defeat.

The Baltimore Orioles, as they convincingly demonstrated in the league championship and the World Series, were the best team in baseball by a large margin, and there was no shame in losing to them. As a team, the Yankees had changed a lot since spring training, and a number of the individual players had grown considerably. But Steinbrenner, casting about for someone to blame when things didn't go precisely his way, was the same man he'd been in Fort Lauderdale, when he announced that the National League umpires were part of a conspiracy that was somehow out to get him. He hadn't changed at all.

< 168 >

Afterword

The season had barely ended when Steinbrenner was once again in court, this time trying to block Commissioner Bowie Kuhn's right to hold disciplinary hearings about his attempts to block the completion of the pine-tar game. Steinbrenner claimed that Kuhn's record demonstrated the commissioner was so biased against him that he couldn't get a fair hearing. After two sessions, however, Steinbrenner dropped the attempt, and hearings were held in Kuhn's office on December 12 and 19. The results of those hearings were initially announced by the Yankees—at 11:30 on the Friday night before Christmas. Steinbrenner escaped suspension but was hit with a $250,000 fine, the largest in Kuhn's tenure.

This, however, was perhaps the least of the Yankee owner's troubles, for by then Gossage had announced that he had no desire or intention to "play for George Steinbrenner." Gossage's decision was a direct result of the mightily anticipated action Steinbrenner finally got around to taking on December 16: he fired—"shifted" is what he insisted at the press conference—Martin and named Yogi Berra manager. Though Steinbrenner had apparently reached his decision shortly after the end of the season—he'd told a meeting of the limited partners that Martin was gone—the process had been tortuously

< 169 >

drawn out. On November 1, he promised a decision "within ten days"; on November 11, he said, "I'll get it done before Thanksgiving Day"; and shortly after Thanksgiving, he promised, "I'll get it done soon. It's not fair to anybody not to get it done."

In fact, the charade dragged on all through major league baseball's winter meetings, which for Yankee watchers became a performance of "Waiting for Yogi," and by the time Berra was officially named, the Yankees had taken several other actions that virtually guaranteed that his roster decisions would be at least as difficult as those that had faced Martin in the spring of '83. Though the outfield crush had eased when Oscar Gamble opted for free agency (and might well be solved entirely if Piniella fails to recover from his illness), the left side of the infield was now ludicrously overcrowded. The Yankees had re-signed Nettles to a two-year contract, traded with the Angels to get shortstop Tim Foli, negotiated a contract extension with Smalley, and were at least publicly confident that Andre Robertson would be back. In addition, they'd acquired catcher Mike O'Berry but had traded neither Cerone nor Wynegar nor Espino. Finally, though they'd traded Roger Erickson and Curt Kauffman, easing their bullpen traffic jam somewhat, they'd also acquired Mike Armstrong, the winning pitcher in the pine-tar game but hardly a Gossage.

On the day he appointed Berra, Steinbrenner didn't seem at all worried about any of these problems, and announced that the team's "number one priority" was re-signing Gossage, "which I'm confident we'll be able to do." Early the next week, he sent Gene Michael, the former manager and future third-base coach, and Jeff Torborg to San Diego to meet with Gossage and his agent, Jerry Kapstein. Before any negotiations could take place, however, Gossage issued a blistering statement saying that he no longer wanted to "play for George Steinbrenner" and that he'd instructed his agent not even to entertain offers from the Yankees. The statement—which referred to "Mister Torborg," "Mister Michael," and "Mister Kapstein," but pointedly omitted the honorific in the two references to "Steinbrenner"—was a typical Gossage high hard one, and its import was unmistakable: by spreading the story that Gossage would refuse to come back if Martin was manager, Steinbrenner had tried to make the pitcher the cause for his decision to fire Martin. But Gossage wasn't playing. For the

< 170 >

first time in his reign, Steinbrenner had lost a Yankee he wanted to keep.

The absence of Gossage would of course make Berra's job considerably more difficult—a matter of no small concern to Yankee fans—but perhaps the greatest significance of Gossage's decision was that, when coupled with Kuhn's precedent-shattering fine, it demonstrated that Steinbrenner's act was beginning to work against him. His maneuvering had cost him not only a quarter of a million dollars but also the league's outstanding relief pitcher. Steinbrenner himself, however, seemed unwilling or by now was perhaps even unable to read the message Gossage had so clearly sent. "I think Goose didn't want to come back here because the fans were so unfair to him last year," said Steinbrenner blandly. Hearing that, one could only conclude that however different the Yankees' 1984 cast might be, it was doomed to appear in the same George Steinbrenner production.

< 171 >